THE ROMAN EMPIRE THE EMPIRE OF THE EDOMITE.

WILLIAM BEESTON

Martino Fine Books
Eastford, CT
2019

Martino Fine Books
P.O. Box 913,
Eastford, CT 06242 USA

ISBN   978-1-68422-324-4

Copyright 2019
Martino Fine Books

Cover Design Tiziana Matarazzo

Printed in the United States of America On 100% Acid-Free Paper

THE ROMAN EMPIRE THE EMPIRE

OF THE EDOMITE.

WILLIAM BEESTON

LONDON:

(FOR THE AUTHOR),

GEORGE COX, 18 KING STREET, COVENT GARDEN.

1853.

"IF THE WHOLE SCHEME OF SCRIP-
" TURE EVER COMES TO BE UNDERSTOOD,
" BEFORE THE RESTITUTION OF ALL
" THINGS, AND WITHOUT MIRACULOUS
" INTERPOSITIONS, IT MUST BE IN THE
" SAME WAY AS NATURAL KNOWLEDGE
" IS COME AT: BY THE CONTINUANCE
" AND PROGRESS OF LEARNING AND
" LIBERTY; AND BY PARTICULAR PER-
" SONS ATTENDING TO, COMPARING,
" AND PURSUING, INTIMATIONS SCAT-
" TERED UP AND DOWN, WHICH ARE
" OVERLOOKED AND DISREGARDED BY
" THE GENERALITY OF THE WORLD."—
*BISHOP BUTLER'S ANALOGY OF RELI-
GION TO THE CONSTITUTION AND
COURSE OF NATURE.*

THE ROMAN EMPIRE, &c.

In the first year of the reign of Belshazzar king of Babylon, the prophet DANIEL had a dream, and visions of his head upon his bed. " I saw," writes the prophet,* " in my vision by night, and behold the four winds of heaven strove upon the great sea, and FOUR BEASTS came up from the sea, diverse one from another. THE FIRST was like a LION, and had eagle's wings. And behold, another beast, A SECOND, like to a BEAR ; and it raised itself up on one side; and it had three ribs in the mouth of it, between the teeth of it. After this, I beheld, and lo ANOTHER, like a LEOPARD, which had upon the back of it FOUR WINGS OF A FOWL; this beast had also FOUR HEADS. After this, I

* Dan. vii.

saw in the night visions, and behold a FOURTH
BEAST, dreadful and terrible, and strong exceedingly; and it had great iron teeth : it devoured, and
brake in pieces, and stamped the residue with the
feet of it : and it was DIVERSE FROM ALL THE
BEASTS THAT WERE BEFORE IT; and it had
TEN HORNS. I saw in the night visions, and behold, ONE LIKE THE SONS OF MEN came
with the clouds of heaven, and came to the AN-
CIENT OF DAYS, and they brought HIM near
before HIM. And there was given HIM dominion,
and glory, and a kingdom; that all peoples, nations,
and languages should serve HIM * * * *
I came near unto one of them that stood by, and
asked him the truth of all this. So he told me, and
made me know the interpretation of the things.
These great beasts, which are four, are FOUR
KINGS which must arise OUT OF THE EARTH.
The fourth beast will be the FOURTH KING-
DOM UPON EARTH; which will be DIVERSE
FROM ALL KINGDOMS, and will devour the
whole earth, and will tread it down, and break it in
pieces. But the judgment will sit, and his dominion will be taken away; and the kingdom, and
dominion, and the greatness of the kingdom under

the whole heaven, will be given to the PEOPLE OF THE SAINTS OF THE MOST HIGH; whose kingdom is an everlasting kingdom, and all dominions must serve and obey HIM."

The THREE FIRST BEASTS, or the empires of THE BABYLONIANS, THE PERSIANS, and THE MACEDONIANS, having successively passed away, the FOURTH BEAST, or KINGDOM, of the prophecy stood revealed in the iron domination of THE ROMANS; and to the consequent enquiry, WHENCE CAME THE ROMANS? that people have insisted on replying, in the words of their great poet, "AB ORIS TROJÆ: GENUS UNDE LATINUM; ALBANIQUE PATRES; ATQUE ALTÆ MŒNIA ROMÆ."

ÆNEAS,* escaping from the destruction of Troy, after many adventures and dangers, arrived in Italy, where he was kindly received by LATINUS, the king of THE LATINS, who gave him his daughter in marriage. ÆNEAS built a city, which was called LAVINIUM, in honour of his wife. ASCANIUS, his son, succeeded to the kingdom, and to him SILVIUS, a second son; and the succession continued for more than three hundred years in the

Goldsmith's Roman History.

family ; NUMITOR, the fifteenth from Æneas, being the last king. ROMULUS and REMUS, the grandsons of Numitor, resolved to build a town upon the hills where they had lived as shepherds; and, REMUS being slain, ROMULUS laid the foundations of that city which was one day to give law to the world. It was called ROME."

*   *   *   *

But this tradition, which commanded the implicit belief of the Romans themselves, and was held by them in almost religious reverence, has by the learned of our own times been rejected and discarded; and the story of a Trojan colony in Latium is now denounced as fabulous, poetical, and DESTI-TUTE* OF THE SLIGHTEST FOUNDATION IN HISTORICAL TRUTH. Still, the critical acumen which has been found powerful to destroy, has proved impotent to construct; it has deprived us of the ancient faith, but it does not offer us a better creed: at the present hour, all is confusion and conjecture; and the story of the foundation of Rome, and the people from whom THE ETERNAL CITY sprung, are admitted to be the very points about which the learned are most ignorant.†

* Niebuhr.   † Ibid.

Unspeakable, then, must our astonishment be, when we perceive, that this grand secret was certainly discovered, and disclosed, more than twelve hundred years ago; that the true answer to the question WHENCE CAME THE ROMANS? may have been returned, and even registered in writing, before the birth of Christ; that the response proceeded neither from Greek nor Roman, but from the DESPISED JEW; that it has been preserved to us in the JEWISH TARGUMS; that it exists amidst the fables and impieties, the absurdities and the blasphemies, of the JEWISH TALMUD; and that it may be comprehended in these twenty words: THE ROMANS CAME FROM ESAU, WHO IS EDOM; AND ITALY IS THE IDUMEA, ROME THE BOZRAH, OF THE HEBREW PRO-PHETS.

* * * *

"The descendants of Esau," say the JEWISH RABBINS,* "the sworn enemies of the descendants of Jacob, even to the end of the world, were at first a small nation, inhabiting Mount Seir and the adjacent country, contiguous to the land of Canaan. They were easily confined within their own limits,

* Allen's Modern Judaism; London, 1816.

so long as the Israelites enjoyed a great and formidable empire in Canaan : but, after that the powerful republic of the twelve tribes had been destroyed by the Assyrians and Babylonians, they wonderfully increased in numbers and in strength; extended their dominion in the West; subjugated Italy; founded Rome, and the Roman Empire; and at length entirely overturned the Jewish state, the Second Temple being destroyed by Titus Vespasian; and, professing the religion of Jesus Christ, which they were the first of all nations to embrace, they hold Jacob in captivity till MESSIAH BEN DAVID shall appear." The Rabbins further assert, that the prophecies of the prophets against Esau, Edom, and the cities of Edom, have as yet received but a partial accomplishment; and that they will obtain their fulfilment in the punishment and destruction of ROME CHRISTIAN : they designate the Eternal City IMPIOUS ROME; they denominate her empire the IMPIOUS KINGDOM, or KINGDOM OF IMPIETY; and they believe, that the SON OF DAVID will not come until this IMPIOUS KINGDOM SHALL HAVE BEEN EXTENDED OVER THE WHOLE WORLD.

Such is the TRADITION OF THE RABBINS;

and PAPAL ROME has done her utmost to suppress it: but without success. The two citations following will be sufficient for our present purpose.

In the fourth chapter of the Lamentations of Jeremiah, it is written: " He will visit thine iniquity, O daughter of Edom." The Elder Buxtorf * extracts the paraphrase of this passage given by the Targumist, and translates the Chaldee of the original into Latin, by these words: "Isto tempore visitabo iniquitatem tuam, ROMAM IMPIAM, quæ ædificata es in Italia, et repleta es turbis hominum EX POSTERIS EDOM." And he adds, " Sic editiones duæ primæ Venetæ. In posterioribus, ROMA IMPIA, et sequentia verba, omissa sunt, declinandæ invidiæ causa, relicto spatio exiguo, cui Judæi manu inscribere solent omissa, ut factum in exemplari quod apud me est, et a Judæo care emptum." I have referred to a copy of the first edition of the Biblia Hebraica Rabbinnica, printed by Bomberg at Venice in the years 1517–8 and now in the Bodleian Library at Oxford, and find that it contains the passage as cited and translated by Buxtorf. There is, therefore, every reason to suppose that the reading of the first edition of the Bomberg Bible is the genuine paraphrase of the

* Lex. Chald. Talm. et Rabb. fol. 2228.

Targumist; and that the author of the Targum
from which it is extracted was the true JONATHAN
BEN UZZIEL. He is said by the Jews to have
been a disciple of the famous Hillel; and to have
flourished about one hundred years before the destruction of Jerusalem by the Romans.*

"Volumina Talmudica," writes Schoetgenius,
"jussu Pontificis Maximi expurgata esse, res in vulgus
est notissima. Quia vero editiones antiquæ non
expurgatæ, Venetæ et Lublinensis, sunt rarissimæ,
in gratia eorum qui editiones castratas possident.
singula quæ expuncta sunt hic exponam." He then
goes on to restore the original readings of various
passages of the Talmud which have been thus
mutilated, and amongst them he notices the twenty-
third verse of the seventh chapter of Daniel; where
it is said, that the Fourth Beast "shall devour the
whole earth, and shall tread it down, and break it in
pieces." He here introduces the commentary of
Rabbi Jochanan. "Et comedet omnem terram, con-
culcabit et comminuat eam. Dixit Rabbi Jochanan,
חייבת רומי זו : Intelligitur ROMA PECCATRIX." He
adds, "Editione expurgata, loco רומי, Roma, habent

* Talmud. Cod. Shabbath, cap. i.
† Horæ Heb. et Talmud. tom. ii. 840.

פרס., Persam:" and he goes on to say, "Si vota hic quicquam valerent, ut illud exemplum Talmudis oculis usurpare potuerim, de quo sequentia narrat Michael de la Roche, tomo xiv Memoriarum Britannicarum. Il y a dans le bibliothèque publique d'Oxford, un exemplaire du Talmud de Babylon, imprimé à Venise en dix volumes en folio, lequel appartenoit à Selden. Cet exemplaire avoit été revu, conformement aux ordres de l' Inquisition, par un Capucin, qui a raturé tous les passages touchant le Messie, la Vierge Marie, les Apôtres, et les Evangelistes, et TOUS LES ENDROITS OÙ IL EST PARLÉ DE L'EMPIRE ROMAIN, que le Talmud appelle Malcuth Harasha'a, REGNUM IMPIUM. Ces passages raturés ne sont point lisibles; l'encre a tellement penetré le papier, que l'on ne sauroit même lire les mots de la page opposée." — The Jochanan here mentioned is the famous Rabbin Jochanan Ben Zaccai, of whom it was said, that the glory of wisdom ceased when Jochanan died. His constitutions and sayings are frequently referred to in the Mishna,* which must have been completed, at the latest, by the year of our Lord 189. He was greatly favoured by Titus

* Cod. Succa, cap. iii. 12 ; cap. ii. 5. Cod. Ketuboth, cap. xiii. 1.

Vespasian; and died about two years after the destruction of Jerusalem by the Romans. He is said to have received the traditions from the mouth of Hillel himself.

*　　　*　　　*　　　*

I propose, in the ensuing pages, to establish the certainty of this RABBINICAL TRADITION, and demonstrate the true ORIGIN OF THE ROMAN PEOPLE: first, by the testimony of LINGUAL ANALYSIS; and, secondly, by the evidence of the SURE WORD OF PROPHECY.

*　　　*　　　*　　　*

Rome's builder was a LATIN; the first inhabitants of the city were Latins also, and it was, first as the head and leader, and afterwards as the mistress and sovereign of the CONFEDERATED LATINS, that Rome obtained the empire of the world. Rome's language, too, in all its stages, and in all its changes, was ever called the LATIN TONGUE; a certain proof that her original was neither Oscan, Tuscan, Umbrian, or anything but Latin. Yet, Rome was no colony of Alba, or of any other Latin town. Romulus, gathering together the Latin shepherds inhabiting the 'vastæ solitudines'[*] adjacent to the Tiber, built a

* Liv. lib. i. c. iv.

wall round them; and forthwith Rome was. The new-born city received into her veins a large infusion of Sabine blood: but this was more than compensated, and the Sabine element in her first population over-powered, by the destruction of Alba, and the subjugation of the other Latin States; after which, Rome and Latium were the selfsame thing. The notion of a Tuscan population, mixed with the Latin and the Sabine citizens of Romulus, is a dream. The first Tarquin was, no doubt, a Tuscan: but he entered Rome as a private citizen, disgusted with Tarquinii; and, to obtain Rome's franchise, had to change his name. Neither did the city rise slowly, and from insignificance; or climb by short and painful steps to a place amongst the Latins. The birth and rise of Rome were instantaneous. Like the fabled crop of Cadmus, she sprang from the earth armed to the teeth,* and ready, if not eager, for the fight; and from the first hour of her existence, she lived, and moved, and had her being, in total independence of the neighbour towns, and in avowed rivalry with them all. Whilst, therefore, we designate the Fourth Beast of Daniel's prophecy by the Hebrew words ממשל הרומה, MIMSHAL HAROMAH, τὸ IMPE-

* Liv. lib. i. c. 19.

RIUM ROMANUM; the Greek 'Η ΒΑΣΙΛΕΙΑ ΛΑΤΙΝΗ* will be equally descriptive of Rome's iron rule.

The Romans, then, being Latins, the Latins themselves must, according to our RABBINICAL TRADITION, be Idumeans; and our first business, therefore, lies with the origin, history, and language of the ancient Edomites. To the consideration of these questions I now go on ; observing, in passing, that, using their component letters as numerals, each of these names, MIMSHAL HAROMAH, and HE LATINE BASILEIA, contains the number SIX HUNDRED AND SIXTY-SIX; the NUMBER OF THE NAME of the APOCALYPTIC BEAST, " Here is wisdom," writes St. John : " let him that hath understanding count THE NUMBER (of the name) OF THE BEAST; for it is the NUMBER (of the name) OF A MAN; and his number (the number of his name), is SIX HUNDRED THREESCORE AND SIX."

* * * * *

Forty years old was ISAAC, when he took to wife REBEKAH, the daughter of Bethuel the Syrian ; and, at the age of nearly sixty years, the

* Adam Clarke, Comm. on Rev.

patriarch intreated the Almighty for his wife, because she was barren. And Isaac's prayer was heard and answered: Rebekah conceived; and the children STRUGGLED TOGETHER within her. The circumstance was, evidently, preternatural, and of repeated occurrence; for Rebekah went to inquire of the Lord, and said, " Why am I thus ?" The Divine response was given in the words following. " TWO NATIONS ARE IN THY WOMB, AND TWO MANNER OF PEOPLE WILL BE SEPARATED FROM THY BOWELS; AND THE ONE PEOPLE WILL BE STRONGER THAN THE OTHER PEOPLE; AND THE ELDER WILL SERVE THE YOUNGER." These are the infant struggles of two contending nations, descendants of twin brothers, to whom thou wilt give birth: of these peoples, the one will be greatly stronger than the other; and the descendants of the elder will be made the servants of the younger, brother.

Rebekah's days to be delivered were fulfilled; and, behold, there were twins in her womb. The first came forth all hairy, covered with hair as with a hairy garment; and the HAIR WAS RED. They called him ESAU. The other, in the birth, catches

his elder brother by the heel; and, from that cir-
cumstance, is named JACOB, HE-WILL-TRIP-UP-
(MEN'S)-HEELS. The appellation ESAU has
never, I believe, been interpreted. I take it to be
Syriac; and to be compounded of ܐܹܫ, ES (Hebrew
ܐܵܫ, ESH), FIRE, FLAME, the definite O, and
HU, (HE IS). These words being brought together,
the Zekofo, or O, will change to Pethoco, A; the
HE, or H, will be expelled from the text; and the
vowels A and U will form a diphthong:* thus:
ESOHU, ESAHU, ESAU: A-FIREBRAND-IS-
HE. I have not been able to discover the word, in
the simple form, in the Syriac; but there are, I
think, clear traces of its existence in the earlier
periods of that language. Thus Schindler,† speaking
of the Hebrew ܐܵܫܵܫ, ASHASH, says, "Respexit
ad ܐܵܫ, ESH;" and, accordingly, we find the
Syriac ‡ verb ܐܹܫܸܫ, ASES, INFLAMMAVIT.
The name would, therefore, appear to have been
suggested, not merely by the hairiness of Esau, but
by the colour of his hair; and we learn from
it that this colour was fiery red, SCARLET. We

* Phillips's Syriac Grammar, London, 1837, p 10.
† Lex. Pentaglott. fol. 1653.
‡ Castell. Lex. Syr. cur. I. D. Michaelis, Goett. 1788, page
661. Ibid. ܕܫܟ̈ܡܐ, ܟܡܘܡܪܐ Conflagratio mundi.

seem to be here put into possession of a circumstance of domestic history: the Hebrew father
names one son, and the Syrian mother the other;
and each child derives his appellation from the
naming parent's mother-tongue.

The boys grew: Esau became a cunning hunter, a
man of the field; but Jacob was a plain man, dwelling in tents. Esau was the favourite of Isaac, and
this, because the patriarch did eat of his venison; but
Rebekah's favourite was Jacob. Amongst other
accomplishments of a life which, compared with
Esau's, was sedentary and civilized, Jacob possessed
skill in cookery; he sod (was in the habit, that is,
of sodding,) a certain red pottage, of which Esau
seems to have been particularly fond, and the composition of which Jacob, it appears, kept to himself.
The partiality of Esau for this food proved the turning
point in the fortunes of the predicted nations. "And
Jacob sod pottage. And Esau came from the field;
and he was faint. And he said to Jacob, Feed me,
I pray thee, with that same red pottage; for I am
faint. And Jacob said, Sell me this day thy
birthright. And Esau said, Behold I am at the
point to die: and WHAT PROFIT shall this birthright do to ME? And Jacob said, Swear to me

this day: and he sware unto him; and sold his
birthright to Jacob." "Thus," writes Moses, "did
Esau despise his birthright;" and St. Paul declares
that, so doing, he became a 'profane man.'

Now, this transaction appears to be grievously
misunderstood; and the conduct of Jacob towards
his brother most unjustly condemned. The birthright sold by Esau was the possession (not by himself, but his descendants) of two third-parts of the
promised land; this gift of God to Abraham being
divisible amongst all the sons of Isaac (in whom
alone the patriarch's seed was called) in such manner
as that the eldest son should have the 'double
portion.' It is extraordinary that, with the express testimony of Scripture to the contrary, the
commentators should insist that Esau's birthright
included the future priesthood, and the glory of
becoming the progenitor of the Christ of God.
"Reuben, (writes the author of First Chronicles,*)
was the firstborn of Israel; but, forasmuch as he
defiled his father's bed, his birthright was given unto
the sons of Joseph. But the genealogy (of the chief
ruler) is not to be reckoned after (has no connection
with) the birthright: for (as to this) Judah prevailed

* 1 Chron. v. 1.

above his brethren; and of him (comes, not came)
the chief ruler;" (the Nagid, or Prince; the Messiah;
called by Daniel * Mashiakh Nagid, Messiah the
Prince). The birthright, or second portion of
Reuben, was given to the sons of Joseph; and
Ephraim and Manasseh inherited in Canaan as two
of the tribes of Israel: but the priesthood fell to
Levi; and, "It is evident," writes the author of
Hebrews, "that our Lord sprang out of Judah."
The charge made against Jacob is, then, that seeing
his brother about to perish of hunger, he took
advantage of his distress, and purchased (not for
himself, but for his descendants) the right to inherit
all the promised land. The notion is utterly incre-
dible, and is in direct contradiction of the sacred
text. Esau is dwelling in the tents of Isaac and
Rebekah; the tents of a mighty prince;† supplied
with all the necessaries and all the elegancies of the
nomade life. He returns from a common hunting
excursion; faint indeed, but not dying of hunger:
he asks not for food in general, and to sustain life,
but he requires to be fed with a special delicacy;
'Feed me, I pray thee, with that same red pottage.' He does not part with his expectancies to

---

* Dan. ix. 25. † Gen. xxvi. 12, 18, 14, 16.

preserve existence; but he basely sells the glorious heritage of his children for ' one morsel of meat,' a single mess of this red pottage. ' Skin after skin, yea, all that a man hath will he give for his life:' and, had Esau done no more, the Apostle had never charged him with profaneness. The words ' Behold, I am at the point to die,' refer to the reversionary character of the promised heritage. More than three hundred years had yet to pass, before the seed of Isaac would become entitled to the actual possession of Canaan; and therefore the gift was worth nothing to Esau himself; it will do no more good to ME, says he, than it would, if at this very moment I were about to die. Wherefore, he rejects God's grace; and, caring nothing for his descendants, sells their inheritance for one meal of pottage. The Apostle's charge against him is, that for a morsel of food, which he might well have gone without, he sold his birthright, and despised the gift of God; and Saint Paul draws from the conduct of this eldest son of Isaac a most impressive warning. Be ye not like unto Esau. For each of you, says the Apostle, addressing the Hebrew converts, there is reserved a birthright, a portion in the heavenly Canaan; granted to you by God as of His free gift, through Christ.

If, now, you should go backward, and, for the sake of the gratifications and enjoyments of this life, which are present and momentary, forfeit your claim to the heritage reserved for you in heaven, which is reversionary and afar off, you play the part of Esau; you sell your birthright for a mess of pottage; you become 'profane men.' The temptation, in all probability, originated with Esau himself; and was ordained by the Almighty to prove the man: to show what was in his heart; to cause him to testify against himself that he had no respect to the Divine promises; that he set no value on the gift of God. We may suppose him to have said, What would I not give for a taste of that red pottage! to eat of it I would part with the half of all that I am worth. And Jacob buys the birthright for a trifle: yet h gives the price set upon it by the elder brother. And, doubtless, Jacob's aim was self-protection, and regard for the interests of the chosen seed. For, as Esau had the power of alienating this heritage, he might have sold it to the sons of any other people; and so have made the Moabites, or the Philistines, co-heritors with the seed of Abraham: and Israel, suffering what the Almighty had put it in his power to prevent, would have proved himself as 'profane' a man as was his brother Esau.

The blessing which Esau would afterwards have inherited, and which he then sought with tears, was inseparably annexed to the promised land; and, in consenting to receive it from his father Isaac, Esau was the aggressor, and endeavoured to deprive Jacob of his undoubted right. If we compare the words of this blessing with the terms of that afterwards bestowed on Esau, we prove the fact at once. The DWELLING mentioned in the last, has no place in the former; and this, because the dwelling-place of the chosen seed had been already fixed: "Unto thee, even unto thy seed, will I give all these countries," were the words* of God to Isaac. It is evident, therefore, that the sale of Esau's birthright had been carefully concealed by him from his father; and that Isaac, blessing the elder son, intended to bless the younger also: for, as to one third of Canaan, the inheritance was ever Jacob's. God had given this land to the seed of Isaac: but the Almighty might have laid their heritage waste; or, granting it fertility, have caused it to become the basest of the kingdoms. The blessing which Isaac, by the Spirit

* Gen. xxvi. 3.

of prophecy, was enabled to pronounce, had reference
solely to the character and political importance of
the promised land, and not to its locality. " God
will give thee of the dew of heaven, and of the fatness of the earth, and plenty of corn and wine;
peoples will serve thee, and nations will bow down
to thee; be thou the ruler of thy brethren, and thy
mother's sons shall bow down to thee: cursed is he
that curseth thee; and blessed is he that blesseth
thee." Now, the mode in which Jacob obtained
this blessing was prescribed to him by his mother
Rebekah. "Upon me," said the wife of Isaac, " be
thy curse:" in other words, no curse can follow com-
pliance with my request. Isaac, indeed, 'trembled
with an exceeding great trembling' (as well the
patriarch might), when, for the first time, he learned
that his beloved son had forfeited all title to the
grace of God; and had, as it were, flung the gift of
heaven in the great Giver's face: but, constrained by
the Spirit which spake by him, he forthwith adds,
" Yea, and he must be blessed." In this transaction,
Isaac was the prophet of the Lord; and to impose
upon the patriarch was, therefore, to lie to the Holy
Ghost. The Queen of Israel made the attempt, and
what was the result? " Come in, thou wife of

Jeroboam, why feignest thou thyself to be another?"
were the sightless seer's words. And so with Jacob
and Rebekah. We might expect to hear from Isaac,
'How is it that ye have agreed together to tempt
the Spirit of the Lord? ye have not lied unto man,
but unto God.' Yet, the imposition is not detected;
the punishment of Ananias and Sapphira does not
follow the attempt. Far otherwise: no sooner has
the supposed crime been committed, than we hear
the Almighty approving the deed, and blessing the
chief actor in the fraud. " I am the Lord God of
Abraham thy father, and the God of Isaac: the
land whereon thou liest, to thee will I give it, and
to thy seed: and, behold, I am with thee, and
will keep thee in all places whither thou goest."
Let God be true, and every man a liar: let us
eschew, as manifestly false, all interpretations of
Scripture which impugn the justice and the holiness
of the Lord. The blessing was wholly Jacob's; the
mode in which it was conferred was suggested by
Rebekah: and she did what she did, to spare, as far
as might be, the feelings, and mitigate the sufferings,
of the aged, sightless, Isaac, consequent on the disco-
very of the degeneracy of his favourite son. But
was not Jacob himself among the prophets? And

Isaac said, "Art thou my very son FIREBRAND?
and Jacob said, I AM." "And the house of Jacob
shall be a fire, and the house of Joseph a flame, and
the house of Esau for stubble: for the Lord hath
spoken it."* The answer of Jacob finds its parallels
in the words of God to Abraham, "Take now thy
son, thine ONLY SON, Isaac;" and in those passages † of the writings of Saint Paul, and of Josephus,
where Isaac is denominated the patriarch's ONLY-
BEGOTTEN SON. Ishmael and Esau being both
cast out, Jacob became the only-begotten son of
Abraham and Isaac, the sole inheritor of the
promises of the Lord; and his title to the name
'Firebrand' was already registered in the decrees
of God.

But the great and exceeding bitter cry of Esau,
"Hast thou but one blessing, O my father? bless
me, even me also," was both heard and answered
by the Almighty: the Spirit of prophecy descended
upon Isaac for the second time; and the destinies
of the sons of Esau were revealed. "Behold, thy
DWELLING shall be of the FATNESS OF
THE EARTH, and of the DEW OF HEAVEN

---

* Obad. 18.
† Heb. xi. 17 ; Joseph. Antiq. lib. i. c. 13, 1.

from above; and by THY SWORD SHALT THOU
LIVE; and thou shalt SERVE THY BRO-
THER; and it shall come to pass, CAASHÈR
TARÌD, that thou shalt break his yoke from off thy
neck." I quote a part of this prophecy in the original
Hebrew; because the word TARÌD is susceptible of
two widely-differing interpretations. First, with the
Jewish commentators, we may derive this word from
RADAH, DOMINARI: " And it shall come to
pass that, when THOU SHALT HAVE THE
DOMINION, thou shalt break his yoke from off
thy neck." TARÌD may also be deduced from
RUD, TO WANDER ABOUT, TO WANDER
FAR AWAY: "And it shall come to pass that,
WHEN THOU SHALT BECOME A WAN-
DERER, thou shalt break his yoke from off thy
neck." It is evident that there is nothing in the
history of the Edomites, as hitherto understood, by
which this portion of the prophecy can possibly have
been accomplished: but, if the Æneas of the Roman
story and his followers, if the whole Latin people,
were Idumeans, then this great prophecy has been
fulfilled in both the meanings put upon the word
TARID. Now, we learn from Dionysius of Halicarnassus, that all did not admit that this Æneas

was a Trojan." "Some historians," says Dionysius,[*] " affirm that Æneas (the Æneas of Homer) did not even come into Italy; and some, that he (the Æneas who did come) was another Æneas, not the son of Venus and Anchises."

The expectations of Rebekah were fulfilled: Esau's anger passed away; and we find him meeting Jacob, on the return of the latter from Padan-Aram, in perfect amity and peace. "And Esau ran to meet him, and embraced him, and fell upon his neck, and kissed him; and they wept." The reconciliation of the two brothers was complete. They afterwards buried their father Isaac in the sepulchre of Abraham, in the field of Machpelah, before Mamre; and thereupon Esau retired from Canaan, and "from the face of his brother Jacob, and dwelt in Seir: for their riches were more than that they might dwell together; the land wherein they were strangers could not bear them, because of their cattle."

On the approach of Esau, Jacob obtained from the Almighty the great name ISRAEL; an appellation which contains the prophetic history of the Jewish race. The patriarch at first supposed the intentions of his brother towards him to be hostile: and " he

* Antiq. Rom. lib. i. c. 53.

was greatly afraid and distressed; and he divided the people that was with him, and the flocks, and the herds, into two bands; and he said, If Esau come to the one company, and smite it, then the other company which is left may escape." "And Jacob was left alone; and there wrestled a man with him until the breaking of the day. And when he saw that he prevailed not against him, he touched the hollow of his thigh; and the hollow of Jacob's thigh was out of joint, as he wrestled with him. And he said, Let me go, for the day breaketh; and he said, I will not let thee go, except thou bless me." Then the DEITY discovers Himself. "And HE said unto him, What is thy name? and he said, JACOB," HEEL-TRIPPER; I have no better name. "And HE said, Thy name shall no more be called Jacob, but ISRAEL," (AS-)GOD-SHALL-HE-WRESTLE; " KI SARÌTHA IM ELOHÌM, VEÌM ANASHÌM VATTUCAL :" "FOR WITH GOD HAST THOU WRESTLED, AND WITH MEN MUST THOU PREVAIL." He that has wrestled with God, without being thrown, must needs be victorious in all his wrestlings with mankind. The name is compounded of יִשְׂרֶה, ISRÈ, HE SHALL WRESTLE, and אֵל, EL, GOD; the Caph of similitude, or the word

' AS,' being understood, and the Segol (or E) of the verb changed into Kamets, (the long A,) as the sign of the proper-name, and in accordance with a rule hereafter to be stated. ISRE-EL, ISRAÈL, AS-GOD-SHALL-HE-WRESTLE. Both the patriarch's names are agonistic terms; and each of them is the opposite of the other. JACOB is the wrestler who, inferior to his adversary in strength, makes up for the deficiency by his adroitness; and so ' supplants,' that is, ' trips up,' his opponent: ISRAEL is the wrestler who at once lifts his antagonist off his legs, and hurls him backward to the earth. Do we seek a Scripture commentary on this great name? We have it in the speech of Zeresh and the wise men to Haman :* " If Mordecai be of the seed of the Jews, (the CONFESSORS-OF-JEHOVAH, for such is the interpretation of the word Judahite, or Jew,) thou wilt not prevail against him, but wilt surely fall before him." The signification of the name JACOB has been greatly obscured by our translators, through the use of the more learned term ' supplant.' " And Esau said, Is he not rightly named Jacob? these two times hath he tripped up my heels: he took away my birth-right; and now hath he taken

* Esth. vi. 13.

away my blessing." And Jacob called the name
of that place PENIEL, (פניאל), and PENUEL,
(פנואל), GOD-HATH-LOOKED-GRACIOUSLY :
"for," said he, "I have seen God face to face,
and my life has been preserved."

The subsequent history of the Edomites of the East,
so far as it has been recorded, may be related in few
words: we know, indeed, little more of their history *
than as it is connected with that of the Jews. They
were smitten by Saul, in the earlier part of his reign,
or about the year 1087 before Christ.† About the
year 1044 before Christ,‡ David and his captains made
an entire conquest of the Edomites; slew many
thousands of them; compelled the rest to become his
tributaries and servants; and planted garrisons among
them to secure their obedience. In this state of ser-
vitude they continued about one hundred and fifty
years, or to the year before Christ 889. In the days
of Jehoram, § the son of Jehoshaphat King of Judah,
they revolted, and recovered their liberties, and made
a king over themselves; but afterwards, Amaziah
King of Judah, slew of Edom, in the Valley of Salt

* Bishop Newton on the Prophecies.
† 1 Sam. xiv. 47.
‡ 2 Sam. viii. 14; 1 Kings xi. 16; 1 Chron. xviii. 13.
§ 2 Kings viii. 20.

ten thousand, and took SELAH by war,* and called the name of it JOKTEEL: and other ten thousand, left alive, did the children of Israel carry away captive, and brought them unto the top of the rock (whereon Selah was built), and cast them down from the top of the rock, so that they were all broken in pieces.† Amaziah's son, Uzziah, took from them Elath, that commodious haven on the Red Sea, and fortified it anew,‡ and restored it to Judah. Judas Maccabeus attacked and defeated them several times;§ killing, on one occasion, no fewer than twenty thousand, and more than twenty thousand on another: he took their chief city, Hebron, and the towns thereof, and pulled down the fortress of it, and burned the towers thereof round about. At last, his nephew Hyrcanus, the son of Simon, took others of their cities, and reduced them to the necessity of embracing the religion of the Jews, or of leaving their country, and seeking new habitations elsewhere: whereupon they submitted to be circumcised; became proselytes to the Jewish creed; and were incorporated with the church and nation of the Jews.‖ They were swal-

* 2 Kings xiv. 7.   † 2 Chron. xxv. 12.
‡ 2 Kings xiv. 22.
§ 1 Macc. v. 65; 2 Macc. x. 15, 17, 18, 23.
‖ Joseph. Antiq. lib. xiii. c. 9. 1.

lowed up, and lost, partly among the Nabathean
Arabs, and partly among the Jews; and the very
name of Edomite was abolished, and disused, about
the end of the first century after Christ. 'And
where,' asks Bishop Newton, 'is the name or the
nation now?' The TRADITION OF THE RAB-
BINS bids us go west, to Italy, and find the sons of
Esau; there called THE LATINS.

And here a question of the last importance presents
itself to our consideration. Does the prophetic blessing pronounced by Isaac in favour of Esau and the
Edomites remain to be accomplished; or, has Heaven
withheld from us the testimony required to make
good the proof of its fulfilment? If there were
no Edomites save the Idumeans of the East, we shall
be driven to the affirmation of one of these alternatives; since signal failure has attended all attempts
to sustain the accomplishment of the prediction by
the records of the history of the Edomites of the East.
" Behold, thy dwelling shall be of the FATNESS
OF THE EARTH, and of the DEW OF HEAVEN
from above." " The prophecy of Malachi," says
Bishop Newton, " which is commonly alleged as a
proof of the barrenness of the country, is rather an
argument to the contrary; for this implies that the

country was fruitful before; and that its present un-
fruitfulness was rather an effect of war and devasta-
tion than any natural defect and failure in the soil."
On the words, "AND BY THY SWORD SHALT
THOU LIVE," the Bishop remarks: "Esau himself
might be said to live much by the sword; for he was
a cunning hunter, and man of the field; and he and
his children gat possession of Mount Seir by force
and violence, by destroying and expelling from thence
the Horites, the former inhabitants." If we carefully
examine the prophecy of Malachi, we shall be satis-
fied that it refers to the original sterility of Seir, and
describes the condition of the country as it existed
when the Almighty gave it to the Edomites. "Was
not Esau Jacob's brother? saith the Lord: yet I loved
Jacob and hated Esau; and I laid his mountains and
his heritage waste, for the dragons of the wilderness."
To say of a cunning hunter that he was a swordsman,
and of a man of the field that he lived by his sword,
would seem to be a perversion of language as gross
as it would be to designate the battles and sieges of a
Marlborough, or a Wellington, fox-huntings and
battues; and the title of the children of Edom to
Mount Seir was precisely that by which the sons
of Israel claimed Canaan. " I gave Mount Seir unto

Esau for a possession." "As the Lord did to the children of Esau, which dwelt in Seir, when he destroyed the Horites from before them; and they succeeded them, and dwelt in their stead, even unto this day." It is not said of the Israelites, that they lived by the sword; and, therefore, something beyond the mere making of war, which is common to all nations, must have been intended by the prophet when he applied these words to the predictive history of the house of Esau. The further observation of the Bishop becomes, when opposed to the RABBINICAL TRADITION with which we have to do, a mere begging of the question. "Esau," he says, "solicited a blessing; and the author of the Epistle to the Hebrews,* tells us that Isaac blessed both Jacob and Esau: whereas, had he consigned Esau to such a barren and wretched country, it would, rather than a blessing, have been a curse." Doubtless, Esau would have preferred a more fruitful field to dwell in: nevertheless, he inhabited Mount Seir; and, so doing, obeyed the declared will of God.

But, if rejecting these, and such-like interpretations, as wholly unworthy of reception, we can assign an Idumean origin to the Latin people, we at once

* Chap. xi. 20.

discover that this great prophecy, like every other fulfilled prophecy of God, has been accomplished to the very letter, and in the fulness of the letter, of its terms. " Behold THY DWELLING shall be of the FATNESS OF THE EARTH, and of THE DEW OF HEAVEN from above." To place the reader in full possession of the glowing description of Italy given by Dionysius,* it would be necessary to transcribe nearly the whole of two of the chapters of his ROMAN ANTIQUITIES. In his opinion, Italy excelled in fertility, not merely the countries of Europe, but those of every other portion of the world; not excepting even Egypt, Libya, and Babylonia. He speaks particularly of the ' fatness of the earth,' the corn-lands, producing as much as three crops in a single year; and, as if referring to the very prophecy we are now considering, he notices the ' dew of heaven from above,' the dewiness and moisture of the herbage, which kept the cattle feeding on it always in good condition. Then, he describes the happy temperature of the climate, suiting itself to every season; so that neither the formation of fruits, nor the constitution of animals, were in the least injured by excessive

* Lib. i. cap. 36, 37.

cold or heat; and, lastly, he affirms that the plains below Alba (the central city * of the Latins), were beautiful to the eye, rich in the produce of all sorts of fruit, and in no degree inferior to the other parts of Italy. " AND BY THY SWORD SHALT THOU LIVE." The Romans were, perhaps, the very people of whom it might most justly be predicated that they ' got their living ' by the sword. " War," said the elder Cato, " is the business of the Roman people." " As the Romans themselves relate," said Mithridates,† " that they were nourished by the dugs of a wolf; so all that people have the disposition of wolves, never to be satiated with blood and power, greedy and hungry after riches." And Minucius Felix: ‡ " Whatever the Romans hold, cultivate, or possess, is a prey won by profligate boldness: all their temples are erected out of the ruins of cities, and the plunder of the gods." " AND THOU SHALT SERVE THY BRO-THER." This portion, and only this portion of the prophecy, was certainly accomplished by the Edom-ite of the East. " And it shall come to pass WHEN THOU SHALT WANDER FAR AWAY, WHEN

* Strabo. † Justin. lib. xxxviii. cap. 6.

‡ Octav. cap. xxv.

THOU SHALT HAVE THE DOMINION, that thou shalt BREAK HIS YOKE from off thy neck." To what part of the history of the Edomites, yet ascertained, will we refer these words for their fulfilment? When did Esau obtain dominion? When did he wander from Mount Seir; and whither, in his wanderings, did he go? Yet, (Rome's Idumean origin admitted,) what prophecy ever received accomplishment more literal and complete? In the destruction of Jerusalem, and the subjugation of Judæa and the Jews, this acknowledged MISTRESS OF THE NATIONS, did indeed break off the yoke imposed by Jacob on her neck.

Guided, then, by the words of Scripture, and the TRADITION OF THE RABBINS, let us now turn westward, and seek the Edomites of Isaac's prophecy on Italian ground.

* * * *

The great question which presents itself at the outset of all inquiries into the antiquities of the Roman history, is, Whether * the TROJAN LEGEND be ancient and home-sprung; or whether it originated with, and was obtained by the Romans from, the Greeks. The result of the laborious and

* Niebuhr.

most satisfactory inquiries of Niebuhr on this point
may be compressed into small space. " The
story," he says, " that the Trojans were not utterly
destroyed at the fall of Troy, but that a part of them
survived, and that this remnant had been governed
by the house of Æneas, is as old as the Homeric
poems. But the Trojans under Æneas, even according to the account which assigns them the greatest
importance, were not an immigrating tribe, such
as would alter the people it unites with. In the
earliest Roman accounts, they are represented as
the crew of a single ship; and even in the later
narrative they are still no more than a small band,
for whom the fields of a single village would
suffice. But the passage in the Twentieth Book of
the Iliad * would more naturally refer the prophecy
to the occupation by Æneas, and the independent
Dardanians, of the desolated territory of Ilium after
the departure of the Greeks; and, accordingly,
Aretinus of Miletus, a poet contemporary with
the building of Rome, says that Æneas and his
followers retired to Mount Ida. Now, if the

---

* For Priam, now, and Priam's faithless kind,
  At length are odious to th' all-seeing mind :
  On great Æneas shall devolve the reign ;
  And sons succeeding sons the lasting line sustain.
  Pope's Iliad, Book xx., lines 353-356, and the note.

Milesian poet, whose great antiquity Dionysius of Halicarnassus expressly urges, had related anything about a subsequent emigration of Æneas, it is inconceivable that Dionysius should have rejected his evidence, when he was amassing all that he could muster out of Hellanicus, Cephalon, and other writers so much more recent. After the middle of the fifth century of Rome, Callias adopted the story of the Trojans settling in Latium, and uniting with the Aborigines, which he indicates by the marriage of Roma with King Latinus. Soon afterwards, Pyrrhus crossed over into Italy; and Pausanias * held the notion that he felt himself called upon, as a descendant of Achilles, to wage war with the Romans, as a Trojan colony; this notion being, in all probability, borrowed from some contemporary writer, Hieronymus or Timæus. From this time forward, the belief in the Trojan colony became universal amongst the Greeks: it was professed by Eratosthenes in the first half of the next century; and it is only by mere accident that we possess no Greek work in which it is expressed more ancient than the Lycophron of Cassandra, written about the year of Rome 560. Whatever

* Att. cap. 12.

use learned Romans, in the age of Augustus, might make of Greek poets, to show that the tradition was known early to the Greeks, it is extremely improbable that a belief concerning its origin, adopted by the whole nation, should have been borrowed from abroad; above all, it is improbable that a belief of this kind should be of foreign origin when recognized by the state, a state so proud, and so contemptuous towards every thing foreign, as was Rome. That it was so recognized, we find remarkable proofs, in collecting the earliest traces of the Trojan legend amongst the Romans; proofs drawn from times when Greek literature had certainly not found admission, except with a few individuals. The first transaction between the Greeks and the Romans was the application of the Roman Senate to the Ætolians for the freedom of the Acarnanians, on the plea that the Romans were bound to protect those whose ancestors alone, of all the Greeks, took no share in the war against their progenitors, the Trojans. This embassy must not be dated before the year of the city 509, nor later than 515 or 516. About the same time, the Senate wrote a letter to King Seleucus Callinicus, who reigned after the year of Rome 509, demanding, as the condition of their entering into a treaty of friendship and alliance with him, that the Ilians, the kinsmen of the Roman people, should be exempted from tribute. The Ilians were also included by the Romans in their first treaty of peace with Macedonia, in the year of the city 549. Fifteen years afterwards, when the Scipios crossed the Hellespont, the Ilians boasted of their affinity with the Romans, and called them their colony: the Romans were delighted to see their mother-country; and the consul offered sacrifice in the citadel to Athene. The appeal was dishonest: for these Ilians were originally an Æolian colony, mixed by the kings of Macedonia (who at one time enlarged the city, and at another changed its site), with a concourse of people taken out of various nations." "The Trojan legend was not brought into Latium by Greek literature; but must be considered home-sprung."

Such is the result of the inquiries and investigations of Niebuhr; and from these premises the historian draws a conclusion, the very last at which he might have been expected to arrive. "In spite," says he, "of the fact that the Trojan legend was not brought into Latium by the Greeks, but must be considered home-sprung, it has not the

SLIGHTEST FOUNDATION IN HISTORI-
CAL TRUTH; nor has it even the slightest
HISTORICAL IMPORTANCE.   A belief of
this sort does not require long to become a national one, in spite of the most obvious facts, and
the clearest historical proofs to the contrary; and
then, thousands would be ready to shed their
blood for it: they that would introduce it, need
but tell people roundly that it is what their fore-
fathers knew and believed; only the belief was ne-
glected, and sank into oblivion." Well may reason-
ing of this kind cause us to start.

The Trojan legend, as Niebuhr himself con-
fesses, was a national belief; that is (for the pro-
position must be qualified by the testimony of
Dionysius, before cited*), it was the persuasion of
the great majority, though not of the entirety, of the
Roman people: all concurred in deriving the origin
of the nation from an Æneas; and the most part
(amongst them Dionysius), held that this Æneas
was the Æneas of Homer, the son of Venus and
Anchises.   We have here a proud and powerful
people, good haters of all foreigners, giving evidence against themselves; and yet we must refuse

* Page 29.

them our belief. Nations have ever wished and
tried to make themselves out aborigines, autochthones, not outcasts and defeated wanderers: but
the Romans must not be listened to, when, spite of
this most natural inclination, they cling to the
persuasion that the founders of their race, their
own Æneas and his followers, were helpless,
homeless fugitives, "Cremata patria et domo *
profugi, sedem, condendæque urbi locum, quæ-
rentes." "What cause," exclaims Dionysius,†
"can be assigned for the monuments erected to
Æneas in Italy, if he never reigned in those parts,
resided there, or was entirely unknown?" And,
with the Translator of the same historian, Spelman,‡
we may well retort, that to reject the tradition is
'an attempt to transform all history into romance;
to destroy the use, by destroying the credit, of it;
and to deprive mankind of the best guides both in
public and private life, examples.'

But, let us test the credit of the legendary history
of Rome by the application to it of the rules laid
down by Leslie,§ and see how much it offers to
us of that evidence on the faith of which even

---

* Liv. lib. i, c. 1.   † Lib. i., cap. 54.
‡ London, 1758, vol. i., p. 216.
§ Short Method with the Deists, Lond. 1699.

miracles must be admitted and believed. The
rules are: first, that the matter of fact be such,
as that men's outward senses, their eyes and ears,
may be the judges of it; secondly, that the fact
be done publicly, in the face of the world; thirdly,
that not only public monuments be kept up in
memory of it, but some outward actions or observances be instituted and performed; and, fourthly,
that such monuments, and such actions or observances (profess to) be instituted, and to commence
from the time that the matter of fact was done.
Tried by these rules, how little of the antiquities
of the Roman story will remain unproved. The
sacrifice yearly offered by the pontiffs and consuls
to Æneas, as Jupiter Indiges; the Lupercalia; the
Quirinalia; the lifting of the bride over the threshold
of her husband's home; the accompanying cry,
' Talassa;' and the many other rites and outward
actions observed and done in memory and attesta-
tion of the Roman legend, must be got rid of and
disproved, before the story which they affirm is
discarded and sentenced to oblivion, as unworthy
of belief. What, too, is to become of the brazen
wolf, and the cottage of Romulus, preserved to
the times of Nero, if neither wolf nor Romulus
were a chief actor in the tale? False relics

imply true revelation, and owe their value to a confirmed belief. The pretended portions of the cross of Christ, and the Santa Casa of Loretto, pre-suppose unwavering faith in a crucified Saviour, and His virgin mother; and derive their existence solely from this creed. "No human sagacity," says Niebuhr, "can arrive at a decisive solution of the question, What, after all, can have been the origin of the tradition?": nevertheless, aided by the TRADITION OF THE RABBINS, I venture to affirm, that we may establish the certainty of Rome's legendary history by indisputable proofs.

* * * *

The pedigree of the Roman people, as found in Virgil, Livy, Dionysius, and other writers, is enveloped in as thick a darkness, and is as contradictory in itself, as that which at one time covered and distinguished the genealogy of the Roman Jupiter himself. CHAOS gave birth to NOX; from NOX came all things; the eldest of the gods was OURANOS; from Ouranos sprang CHRONOS, otherwise called SATURN; Saturn gave being to divers sons, among them, JUPITER; and JUPITER, or ZEUS, was the FATHER

BOTH OF GODS AND MEN. Such was
the genealogical labyrinth in which the devout
Roman was obliged to walk; and (for he had no
other creed), such were the polytheistic absurdities he was content to reverence and adore. He
worshipped Saturn, the father of the great Jupiter;
he worshipped Jupiter's grandfather, Ouranos;
he worshipped Nox, the first parent of Jupiter
and the rest; he worshipped Jupiter; and him he
worshipped as the FATHER OF GODS AND
MEN. But LIGHT which was TO LIGHTEN
THE GENTILES came from Judea; and mis-
sionaries, issuing from the Holy Land, expostu-
lated with the heathen world, touching the absurdities and contradictions of the Gentile faith.
They taught that in this their Theogony there
existed but a single truth: that their ZEUS,
their JUPITER, by the Jews and by Himself denominated JEHOVAH, was the ONLY GOD;
that by the word of the mouth of JEHOVAH
all things were created, and by the fiat of His
power all things were upholden and preserved; and
that He, theUncreated, Eternal, Infinite, Omni-
potent, and Unchangeable, was the great AUTHOR
of Chaos, and Night, and Day, and Heaven,

and Earth, and Time, and Eternity, Angels, and Men,
and all things else. The vaunted wisdom of the
Greek stooped to be instructed by the Revelation of
the Jew: the Mythology of the ancient world was
thrown aside; and (so to speak) the true Theogony
was established in its place. In like manner, when
Virgil, Livy, and the others, affect to record the
origin and genealogy of the Romans, they involve
themselves in the grossest contradictions; contradictions never, I think, sufficiently noticed, at any
rate, never fairly encountered and disposed of, by
Beaufort, Niebuhr, or any other modern writer
on the subject. At one time, and in one portion
of the writings of the ancients, the whole Latin
people are the descendants of Æneas and his followers; at another, and in a subsequent part of
the same authors, Æneas becomes the adopted
son of King Latinus, and he and his adherents
are received into, and made members of the family
of the Aboriginal Latins. "Genus unde Latinum,
Albanique patres, atque altæ mænia Romæ," writes
Virgil; and, so far, he is intelligible and consistent
with himself. From Æneas, and his band of followers, came the whole Latin race: Alba and the
Albans were the progenitors and head of all the other

E

Latin towns; and from amongst the Albans came
the 'mœnia Romœ;' not the inhabitants, but the
builders, of great Rome. Yet, how completely is
this clear and consistent account of the original
of the Latins contradicted by the contents of the
succeeding books of the Æneid. So Livy : * "Bel-
lum utrimque summa ope parabatur, civili simil-
limum bello, prope inter parentes natosque; Troja-
nam utramque prolem: quum Lavinium ab Troja, ab
Lavinio Alba, ab Albanorum stirpe regum oriundi
Romani essent." And, again :† "Ab eo (Latino
Silvio) coloniæ aliquot deductæ, PRISCI LA-
TINI appellati." And yet it is clear, from the
first chapter of Livy's history, that by the words
" Latinus rex, Aboriginesque, qui tum ea tenebant
loca," he intends to describe the Latin people as
dwellers in Latium from time immemorial, and
as, perhaps, the very Autochthones of the land.
Servius is, I believe, the only writer amongst
the very few that have noticed them, who has
made any attempt at the reconciliation of these
glaring contradictions, and the removal of these
difficulties. All others seem content to take as
certain the statements which make the Latins the

* Lib. i. cap. 23.   † Lib. i. cap. 3.

Aborigines of Latium: but, in doing this, they appear
to forget that it was incumbent on them to reconcile, if possible, the authors of these statements
with themselves. The following is the commentary
of Servius on the words 'genus unde Latinum,'
of Virgil: " Si jam fuerunt Latini, et Latium
dicebatur, contrarium est quod dicit, ab Ænea
Latinos originem ducere. UNDE, adverbium est
de loco; non deductio a persona. Tamen, Cato
in Originibus, dicit hoc: Primo Italiam tenuisse
quosdam qui appellantur Aborigines; hos postea,
adventu Æneæ, Phrygibus junctos, Latinos uno
nomine nuncupatos: ergo, descendunt Latini non
tantum a Trojanis, sed etiam ab Aboriginibus. Est
autem vera expositio hæc. Novimus qui victi,
victorum nomen accipiunt. Potuit, ergo, victore
Ænea, perire nomen Latinum: sed, volens sibi
favorem Latii conciliare, nomen Latinum non
solum illis non sustulit, sed etiam Trojanis imposuit.
Merito, ergo, illi tribuit, quod in ipso fuerat ut
posset perire." But the word UNDE, as an adverb
of place, must, necessarily, refer the origin of the
Latins to the Troy of Priam; that is, to Æneas and
his followers: and Virgil makes the Trojan leader
the guest, not the conqueror, of Latinus and his

subjects: "Dis sedem exiguam patriis litusque
rogamus innocuum, et cunctis undamque auramque
patentem,"* say the Trojans, supplicating Latinus.
The true reason of these contradictory accounts, as
given both by Virgil and by Livy, is apparent. The
current of popular belief ran so strongly in favour
of the opinion which made the whole Latin people
descendants of Æneas and his Trojans, and the
authority of the legends in support of the same
supposition was so great, that these writers were
unable to oppose the two conjoined: at the same
time, they could not reconcile the common story
with the facts, that the very name of Trojan was
no more, and that the Romans were assuredly a
Latin people: wherefore, they placed both these
originals before their readers, and left them to en-
counter the contradictions, thus created, as best they
might. The possibility that the Trojans and the
Latins might be one and the same people, Trojans
inhabiting Latium under the name of Latins, and
so giving that country its name, would seem never
to have occurred, either to the ancients or the
moderns. What the Jews, what the Hebrew prophets and preachers, did for the Theogony of the

* 7 Æ. 229.

Roman, they may be found capable of effecting for the Roman story; by removing this great difficulty, and so revealing the true origin of the Roman people. For, it is manifest that the tradition with which we have to do, must, if true, be referred to a higher antiquity than the days of any of those we commonly call RABBINS, and must derive its original from a far holier source. If JONATHAN BEN UZZIEL, and THE TALMUDISTS, knew the Romans to be Edomites, they had the tradition from their fathers: it must be carried, through the MEMBERS OF THE GREAT SYNAGOGUE, upward to EZRA and the later prophets, at the least; it must be referred to times when (in the language of the Greeks) the gods conversed with men, or (as the Jewish Rabbin would express it) when holy men spake as they were moved by the Spirit of God: the tradition may be as old as the Lamentations of Jeremiah; as old, perhaps, as the prophetic writings of Isaiah.* The study of Roman or Grecian archæology, would find no favour with the Rabbins of whom we speak. To them, the wisdom of the Greeks, mixed as it was with its absurd polytheism, was foolishness, to be detested;

* Isa. lxiii. 1.

Rome, where the congregated gods of all the
GOYIM jostled each other, and fought for rank
and room, was, to these men, the mother of abominations, and the cage of every unclean thing.
Wherefore, as the tradition, if true, must have a
Divine origin; so will its truth be discoverable
by the application of it to the elucidation of the
legendary history of Rome. And, to this I now
proceed.

*　　*　　*　　*

Esau and Jacob spake the same language, the
Hebrew of Moses and the prophets; and this tongue
was also spoken, in all its purity, by the sons of
Jacob, as late, at least, as the destruction of the
First Temple, or for more than one hundred and
sixty years after the foundation of Rome. The same
language may, therefore, have been found with the
children of Esau during the like period; and a very
strong presumption (to say no more), that they
also spoke the Biblical Hebrew, arises from the
fact, that the few names of places and persons
found in their history (as Selah, Bozrah, Job and
his friends, and others) are all Hebrew. Now,
divested of their classical terminations, the names
ÆNEAS, Saturnia, Latini, Latium, TROJA, Lavi-

nium, Alba Longa, ROMA, Ascanius, Silvius, Rhea
Silvia, ROMULUS, Remus, LUPERCUS, Numa
Pompilius, Tarquinius Priscus, DEUS, JUPITER,
JOVIS, Janus, Semo Sancus, Jupiter Latiaris,
Jupiter Feretrius, Jupiter Stator, Quirinus, Satur-
nalia, Quirinalia, Luperca, Lupercal, Lupercalia,
Palilia, Consualia, Templum, Altar, Ara, Sacerdos,
Flamen, CAPITOLIUM, Tarpeia, Rex, Tribus,
Ramnes, Titienses, Luceres, Pater, Senator, Patricius,
Plebs, Patronus, Cliens; all these names, and
almost all the other names, whether of person,
place, or occupation, we meet with in the legendary
history of Rome, are HEBREW: they are all of
them significant in the HEBREW TONGUE;
they tell the tale of Rome; and (being witnesses
above suspicion), they avouch its truth. And the
tale they tell runs (briefly) thus. ENIIAH, also
called SATURNIIAH, and his followers, were
foreigners and fugitives; they fled from fire, and
sword, and bonds, and hid themselves in Italy; they
spoke the HEBREW TONGUE; calling themselves LATINIM, HIDING-(or HIDDEN-)ONES,
in LATION, LATIUM, LATLAND, LAND-OF-
THE-HIDER, they set up their rest; they brought
with them the RELIGION OF THE PATRI-

ARCHS; they worshipped the ALMIGHTY by
His great name JEHOVAH, JHOVAH, JHOVIH,
JOVIS; the God who had redeemed them from the
house of bondage, and made freemen of them in
Italia, they invoked by the name יְהוֹ-פִטֶר, JEHO-
PITTER, JOPITTER, (by subsequent corruption)
JUPITER, JEHOVAII - (THAT) - HATH - SET-
FREE, JEHOVAH-THE ENFRANCHISER; like
the Israelites in Egypt, they mixed not with the
idolaters about them; like the sons of Jacob, from
a small band (some seventy, or a hundred persons), they grew into a nation, and became THE
LATIN PEOPLE; they first built a little town,
which they named TROIAH, and so were called
TROIANIM; they styled themselves LAVINIM,
ADHERENTS, as well as Latins, and the next
town they built they called LAVINION, DWELL-
ING-PLACE-OF-THE-LAVINES; Troiah being
abandoned for Lavinium, the name Trojan ceased,
and was found no more: under Eniiah, Ascani,
and the Silvian kings, these Latins led a peace-
ful, virtuous, godly, happy, life; this was the
GOLDEN AGE of Italy; these the SATURNIA
REGNA, not of the fabled Saturn, but of God's
saint SATURNIIAH, good ENIIAH; RHEA

SILVIA, SIGHTLY SILVIA, gave birth to the twin brothers, ROMULUS AND REMUS; and the shepherd ROMULUS, in his youth, and by his shepherd comrades, called LUPERCUS, WOLF-PRESERVED, built ROME.

Such is the substance of the first part of my argument; an outline of the testimony to the truth of the TRADITION OF THE RABBINS obtainable from an ANALYSIS OF THE OLDEST LATIN. It has next to be expanded and enforced.

* * * *

Jacob and Esau spoke the Hebrew of Moses and the prophets: but was the Biblical Hebrew the mother-tongue of Abraham also? Was it the language brought by the patriarch with him to Canaan, or that found by him on his arrival there; the language of the Canaanites, or Phœnicians, then the inhabitants of the promised land? TEN VERSES (not interpreted) preserved in the PŒNULUS* of PLAUTUS, contained an answer to this question; and, in the year 1850, I obtained from them a text differing but little from the Hebrew of King David and the Books of Kings, and pointed in conformity with the Masoretic punctuation of those books.

* Act v. sc. 1, (Hanno loq.) NYTH ALONIM, &c,

This exposition of the Ten Verses, published in a tract of fifteen pages, is too long to be inserted here; but, as it forms an important step in my argument (and as no copies of the book are now obtainable), I will annex it, by way of Appendix, to the present volume.   It proves, if admitted, the identity of the Phœnician with the Hebrew of the Bible; it shows that the HOLY TONGUE must, like the HOLY LAND, have been derived to the chosen seed through Ham's accursed son, Canaan; and that the sacred text of Moses and the prophets is Phœnician, expressed in the Chaldaic character, which character may, perhaps, have been brought by Abraham from Ur of the Chaldees. If, now, we find the descendants of the Phœnician Dido speaking, in the days of Plautus, the Hebrew of the Israelitish kings, we have strong reasons for believing that the language of the Edomites, when the Trojan Æneas is thought to have fled to Italy, was Hebrew also, or a dialect next door to it. And this supposition receives great support from the fact, that most of the few names of persons and places found in the Scripture history of the Idumeans are clearly Hebrew. Thus: SELAH, Rock; BOZRAH, (perhaps) IMPREGNABLE;

JOB, PERSECUTED - ONE; ELIPHAZ, MY-
GOD - PURIFIETH; ZOPHAR, HASTENER;
ELIHU, HE-IS-MY-GOD, or GOD-IS-MY-GOD,
are all Phœnician, or Hebrew-appellations. But if,
with many of the most learned, we suppose the Book
of Job to have been written by an Idumean, we
at once end the question, and establish the fact.
However, it is unnecessary to pursue the subject
further, since it is quite sufficient, for our present
purpose, to show that the Edomites would very
probably speak the Hebrew, whilst they cannot
be proved to have spoken any other tongue. That
HEBREW was the LANGUAGE of the OLDEST
LATINS, will shortly be made apparent; but
this will not suffice to prove the Latins to
be Edomites. They may have been Canaanites,
Israelites, or some other people speaking the
Phœnician tongue; and the fact that they were
in truth Idumeans, can be established by the evidence of prophecy alone.

"There is no part of the verbal criticism of
the HEBREW TEXT," says Gesenius, "which
opens to us so wide a field as the PROPER-
NAMES; they belong to the small store of
Hebrew which has been handed down to us; and the

existence of many a root is further confirmed by means of them. " This learned Hebraist might have added, that the PROPER - NAMES frequently form a commentary on the history of Scripture, and may be applied by us both in support of the sacred story, and of ancient traditions existing by the side of the inspired text. And these names derive their explanatory powers chiefly from the fact that, whilst they are in themselves significant, they speak the language of the person by whom they are imposed, not of the party on whom they are impressed; the language of the parents who give, not that of the children who receive them. Thus, when God names the chosen seed of Abraham, it is the Almighty Himself who speaks. And thou shalt call his name ISAAC, יִצְחָק, HE-SHALL-LAUGH.* So Hannah: she prayed for a child, and the Lord granted her petition;† wherefore she called his name SAMUEL, שְׁמוּאֵל, HEARD-OF-GOD, HEARKENED-TO-BY-GOD ; thereby proclaiming, that she, Hannah, had been listened to, on this occasion, by the Lord. So

* Gen. xxv. 11; xxvi. 3, 12, 13, 14, 16, 24, 28. Joseph. Antiq. lib. i. cap. 18, 3.
† 1 Sam. i. 27.

the name of David's successor in the throne, SOLO-
MON, שְׁלֹמֹה, SHELOMOH, is an appellation formed
from the participle שָׁלוּם, SHALUM, and the pronoun הוּא, HU, HE. It is the language of David,
and it signifies, PACIFIED-(IS)-HE; that is, the
Almighty, who had pardoned the sins of David,
committed in the murder of Uriah, and his adultery
with Uriah's wife. But the great importance of
this property of the HEBREW PROPER-NAMES
will be best established by the application of it
to a very ancient tradition of the Jews. We read
that on the death of Jehoiakim, King of Judah,[*]
"Jehoiakin his son reigned in his stead, and did
that which was evil in the sight of the Lord, according to all that his father had done." He was,
however, wise enough ' to go out to the king of
Babylon;' and thereby brought himself within
the promise made by Jeremiah; he received ' his
own life for his portion of the spoil' of Jerusalem,
and was carried captive by Nebuchadnezzar to
Babylon, instead of being put to death. In the
thirty-seventh year of his captivity, Evil-Merodach
lifted up the head of Jehoiakin out of prison, and
spake kindly to him; he changed his prison gar-

* 2 Kings xxiv. 6.

ments, and set up his throne above the throne
(rather, set his seat at table above the seats) of
the kings that were with him at Babylon; and he
did eat bread continually before (in the presence
of) the King of Babylon, all the days of his life."
Now, the Jews possess a tradition that this Jechoniah repented him of his sins, and so obtained
mercy with God.   He had a son, called in the
Old Testament SHEALTIEL, in the New, SALA-
THIEL; the father of that Zerubbabel, or Shesh-
bazzar, who became the leader of a portion of
the Jews restored to Jerusalem by virtue of the
edict issued by Cyrus, in the first year of his
reign.   SHEALTIEL, שְׁאַלְתִּיאֵל, signifies, I-HAVE-
SOUGHT-GOD; and SALATHIEL, שַׁלְתִּיאֵל, may
be translated, GOD-HAS-DRAWN-ME-OUT;
to wit, out of my dungeon. We have, I imagine,
in these names, most interesting evidence of the
certainty of the Jewish tradition touching this
Jechoniah; and we may well accept the assurance
they offer us, that this wicked man did, indeed,
turn away from his wickedness, and (by the mercy
of God), save his soul alive.*   In both the appellations given by him to his son, Jechoniah speaks

* Gen. xxxvi. 38.

to his posterity through the child; he testifies his repentance, and receives the favour of Evil-Mero-dach as the gift of God.

Some rules observable in the formation of the PROPER-NAMES of Scripture will next require our attention.

And, FIRST. By a beautiful idiom of the Hebrew, events decreed by the Almighty, and, therefore, certainly to come to pass, are commonly treated, both by Himself and by his creatures, as having actually taken place; so that, in the great majority of cases, the future of prophecy (or certainty) will be expressed by the past tense of the Hebrew verb. The phraseology found in the text next cited runs through all the books of the Old Testament. "It is a light thing that thou shouldst be my servant, to raise up the tribes of Jacob, and to restore the preserved of Israel; I WILL ALSO GIVE (literally, I HAVE ALSO GIVEN) thee for a light unto the Gentiles." * This form of speaking should seem to have originated with the Great Disposer of Events, and is referred to by St. Paul, in his Epistle to the Romans.† "Therefore is it, that it (the promise) is of faith, that it might be by grace:

* Isa. xlix. 6.   † Rom. iv. 16.

to the end the promise might be sure to all the seed; not to that only which is of the law, but to that, also, which is of the faith of Abraham; who before (in the eyes of, κατεναντι,) Him whom he believed, God, WHO QUICKENETH THE DEAD, AND CALLETH THOSE THINGS WHICH BE NOT AS THOUGH THEY WERE, is the Father of us all (the Great Patriarch both of believing Jews and Gentiles): as it is written, A father of many nations HAVE I MADE thee." God, naming Abraham, and making him the father of many nations, used the past tense of the verb; and thereby (writes the Apostle), the Almighty quickened the dead, assured the Patriarch of his resurrection from the dead, and treated the future people as already born. ABRAHAM, says St. Jerome, signifies PATER-VIDENS-POPULUM; literally, PATER-(QUI)-VIDIT-POPULUM; the Patriarch that has beheld, the Patriarch that shall assuredly behold, the " great multitude which no man can number, out of all nations, and kindreds, and people, and tongues," hereafter to stand " before the throne, and before the Lamb, clothed with white robes, and with palms in their hands." The name Abraham is compounded of אב, AB, FATHER, PATRIARCH;

רָאָה, RAAH, HE HAS SEEN; and עַם, AM,
PEOPLE: אַב־רָאָה־עָם, AB-RAAH-AM, אַבְרָהָם
ABRAHAM: THE-PATRIARCH-THAT-HAS-
BEHELD-THE-PEOPLE; THE-PATRIARCH-
THAT-SHALL-ASSUREDLY-BEHOLD-THE-
PEOPLE. And the fulfilment of God's promise,
so far as it respects the resurrection of Abraham
from the dead, is solemnly asserted by our Lord
himself. " Your father Abraham rejoiced, ἵνα ἴδῃ,
ut videret, because he was to see, my day: καὶ εἶδεν,
καὶ ἐχάρη, et vidit, et gavisus est; and he has seen
it, and is glad."*

SECONDLY. In the formation of a proper-name,
and for the purpose of distinguishing the name
itself from the phrase out of which it is formed,
a vowel will commonly be changed. Thus, from
יִצְחַק, ITSKHĂK, we have יִצְחָק, ITSKHĀK, ISAAC,
HE-SHALL-LAUGH; from אֱלִי־שָׁמַע, ELI-SHAMĂ,
אֱלִישָׁמָע, ELISHAMĀ, MY-GOD-HATH-HEARD;
from אֱלִי־שָׁבַע, ELI-SHĀBA, the feminine אֱלִישֶׁבַע,
ELISHĔBA, MY-GOD-HATH-SWORN; from
יִשְׂרָה־אֵל, ISRĔ-EL, יִשְׂרָאֵל, ISRĀEL (AS)-GOD-
SHALL-HE-WRESTLE; from יְהוֹרָאוּדָה, JEHO-
ODĔH, JEHOODĔH, יְהוּדָה, JEHUDĔH, יְהוּדָה,

* John viii. 56.

F

JEHUDĀH, JUDĀH, JEHOVAH-WILL-I-CON-
FESS, CONFESSOR-OF-JEHOVAH. And so on.

THIRDLY. No proper-name is ever formed by
the subtraction from its forming phrase of any
of the pure consonants; that is to say, any of the
letters of the Hebrew alphabet except the six
VOCALES LITERÆ (as Jerome calls * them);
ALEPH, HE, VAU, KHETH, YOD, and AYIN.
These letters, called by the Jews (speaking of
four of them), MATRES (or MATRICES) LEC-
TIONIS, are vowels † as well as consonants; consonants holding within them, as in wombs or
moulds, the vowel sounds of the language, and
being used sometimes as consonants, sometimes as
vowels. The Vocales Literæ, with their vowel-
points, will frequently be expelled from the text,
in the formation of a proper-name; but no one of
the pure consonants is ever thus excluded from the
appellation. A single instance will suffice. There
is scarcely, I believe, a Hebraist who will not
deduce the name JOHN from the Hebrew יוֹחָנָן,
JOCHANAN, JEHOVAH - WILL - BE - GRA -
CIOUS.‡ But the omission of the final NUN, (N),

---

* DE NOMINIBUS HEBRAICIS, &c.

† Joseph. Bell. Jud. v. c. 5, 7.　　　‡ First Rule.

in the Greek Ιωαννης, is fatal to this derivation.
JOCHANAN was a very common name amongst
the Jews, and is always written, in the Greek
of the Septuagint translators, Ιωαναν. The Greek
Ιωαννης is the Hebrew יְהוֹעֶנֶה; formed (as SHĂB-
BĀTH from SHĀBĂTH) by the duplication of
the middle consonant, the change, before the
doubling-dagesh, of the first Kamets into Pathach,
and of the second into Segol (second rule), as the
sign of the masculine noun : יְהוֹעֶנֶה JEHOANNEH,
JOANNEH, JEHOVAH-WILL *- BEGIN-TO-
SPEAK. "But thou,† Bethlehem Ephrathah (thou,
Bethlehem-that-shalt-bring-forth), out of thee shall
He come forth unto me that is to be Ruler in Israel.
Therefore will He give them up (will speak to them
neither by Urim and Thummim, nor by prophets,
nor by dreams), until the time that she which
travaileth (that Bethlehem-Rachel) shall bring
forth." " And ‡ they made signs to his father, how
he would have him called; and he asked for a
writing-table, and wrote, saying, his name is JOHN.
And they marvelled all. And his mouth was
opened immediately; and he was filled with the
Holy Ghost, and prophesied." Well did the Angel

---

* First Rule.   † Mic. v. 2.   ‡ Luke i. 62.

Gabriel announce that, with the circumcision of the Baptist JEHOVAH WOULD BEGIN TO SPEAK; for, even the BENEDICTUS of ZACHARIAS contains an amount of prediction worthy of the chiefest of the prophets.

FOURTHLY. In the formation of a proper-name, the order of the component words will frequently, as in our own and other languages, be inverted. Thus, the Greek 'Ο-ποιος-των-μαχαιρων, A-maker-of-swords, is expressed, both in Greek and English, by a single word: Μαχαιροποιος, SWORD-MAKER. And so in the Hebrew, יְהוּדָה, JEHU-DAH, is אודהיהה, and from אוֹדָה אֶת־יְהֹוָה, Leah forms the name יְהוּדָה יְהוּדָה יְהוֹ־אוֹדָה, JEHUDA. So, יְהוֹאָשׁ, יוֹאָשׁ, JEHOASH, JOASH, is אֵשׁ־יְהֹוָה, LIGHT-(or LAMP)-OF-JEHOVAH.*

FIFTHLY. In Greek and Latin, the final H of the Hebrew will commonly be represented by Σ, or S; which letters, in such case, are mute. Thus, the names of the fourth son of Leah, and of the betrayer of our Lord, are identical; and each of them (JUDAH and JUDAS,) is to be pronounced JUDA. This silent S is supposed to have been derived to the Greeks and Latins from the Sanscrit, in which

* 1 Kin. xv. 4, and Third Rule.

language the sibilant is usually softened into H, by VISARGAH;[*] and it prevails, to a great extent, in the modern French, which seems to have obtained it from the Latin. At first sight, it may not appear easy to establish the identity of the Latin JOVIS and the Hebrew JĔHOVAH: but if we pronounce this name (the S being softened as in the Sanscrit), JOVIH, and reflect that the first vowel of the Hebrew word is short, so that the name readily becomes a dissyllable, JHOVIH, and, further, that with the Latins A is constantly changed into I, we shall find that JOVIS is readily deducible from the JEHOVAH, or JHOVAH, of the Jews.

SIXTHLY. The HE and YOD, or E and I, of the Hebrew, and the E and I of the Latins, have each the sound of our own E, the first of these letters being twice as long as the other of them. Nothing, I apprehend, can be more certain than that the I, as sounded in the English FIRE, has no existence either in the Hebrew, the Greek, or the Latin, when properly pronounced. Indeed, the form of the ' vowel-point' applied by the Punctionists to the Hebrew of the Bible will go far to establish the fact. For, if in the Hebrew, אִישׁ,

---

[*] Wilkins, Sanscrit Gram. pp. 12, 63.

ISH, the KHIRIK is to be pronounced as an E, then the form of the TSERE, in אֵשׁ. ESH, gives a vowel of the same sound, but of twice the length of the first. The modern Jews, indeed, pronounce the TSERE as the French E, in the words PÈRE, and MÈRE; but this seems to be a corruption of the true and ancient pronunciation of the letter; and it was, perhaps, obtained by them from the Greeks: for we find that, in the days of Plato, the Greek ETA had the sound of the English A in PAIN; whilst the earlier pronunciation * of this letter was EE. Traces of the corruption appear in the Greek translation of the Old Testament; in which the INITIAL SHEVA (or SHORT E) of the Hebrew is commonly turned into an A: as SAMUEL for SHEMUEL.

SEVENTHLY. The SHIN, or SH, of the Hebrew was unknown both to the Latins and Greeks; and this letter is always represented, both in Greek and Latin, by the unaspirated S; as SAMUEL for SHAMUEL. We find, indeed, that a large proportion even of the Hebrews were unable to articulate this letter, saying SIBBOLETH for SHIBBOLETH.

* Prof. Black, On the Pronunciation of the Greek Language.

EIGHTHLY. The Hebrews sometimes write the same word with a final HE, or H, and also with a final KHETH, or KH; as קָשָׁה and קָשַׁח, KASHAH and KASHAKH, To be hard; גָּבָה and גָּבַח, GABAH and GABAKH, To be high. On the contrary, an INITIAL KHETH will often, in Greek and Latin, be expressed by an H, or will become altogether mute: as, 'Ερμων, and Hermon, for KHERMON; 'Αννα, and Anna, for KHANNAH.

NINTHLY, and LASTLY. It has been well observed,* that " if it were necessary to describe, in one sentence, the genius and constitution of the Latin tongue, this could not be better done than by defining it to be a language which is always yearning after contraction;" further, that " the cause is to be sought in the strength and prominence of the single accent, which is generally thrown forward as far as possible;" and that " the hasty pronunciation of the Romans, so far as it was exhibited in the written forms of the language, appears chiefly in the omission of syllables in the middle of the words." Now, these are the distinguishing characteristics of the Hebrew also. Few words in that language contain more than three syllables, one of which will

* Donaldson, Varronianus, p. 269.

be shortened; an effort will commonly be made to reduce three syllables into two; and this by the suppression of the middle syllable of the word. Thus, from DĀBĀR (a word), is formed the plural DĔBĀRĪM, (not DĀBĀRĪM); and this plural, when in apposition with another noun, is reduced to a word of two syllables, DIBRĒ (not DĔBĀ-RĪM) KOHELETH, THE WORDS OF THE PREACHER. So, from MĔLĔK (a king), comes the feminine MALKÂH, for MĔLĔKAH; the tone accent falling almost always on the last syllable.

* * * *

To understand the history of ÆNEAS and his companions, considered as the EDOMITES of the TRADITION OF THE RABBINS, and as it is exhibited in the names occurring in the oldest Latin, it will be necessary to review the leading particulars of that system of revealed religion hereinbefore denominated THE RELIGION OF THE PATRIARCHS.

And the old fathers worshipped the ONE TRUE GOD by His name יהוה.* This name the Hebrews for several centuries before the Christian era refused, and still refuse (or, rather, have been

* Gen. xx. 4. Job i. 21. Numb. xxii. 8, 13, 19; xxiii. 3, 8, 12; xxiv. 11, 13. Cic. De Re Pub. lib. i. p. 37 (edit. Heinrich).

forbidden),* to pronounce; and Saint Jerome (who had his Hebrew from the Jewish doctors), writes thus† concerning it: "Prius nomen Domini apud Hebræos quatuor literarum est: י (Iod), ה (He), ו (Vau), ה (He); quod proprium Dei vocabulum sonat, et legi potest IEHOVA, et Hebræi αρρητον, id est ineffabile, opinantur." The great majority of Hebraists, following the opinion of the Jews, suppose that the true pronunciation of the Divine name has, in consequence, been lost; and that the vowel-points attached to it in the Masoretic copies of the Hebrew Scriptures belong to the words ADONAI, and ELOHIM. But, though the Jews for יְהֹוָה, JEHOVAH, substitute, on most occasions, אֲדֹנָי, ADONAI, and, in some cases, to prevent the repetition of ADONAI, אֱלֹהִים, ELOHIM, it does not follow that the true punctuation of יהוה has not been preserved, and is not actually exhibited to us by the pointing יְהֹוָה. First, because the name ADONAI being read by a CONSTANT (or IMPLIED) KERI, it would be sufficient to change the points of יהוה in those cases only where the word ELOHIM was to be used in the place of ADONAI, or where the punctuation of ADONAI was affected

* Joseph. Antiq. lib. ii. 12. 4.   † On Psa. viii.

by prefixes.   Next, because the points actually
affixed to יהוה are not those proper to אדני, but
differ from them in an important particular, the use
of the SHEVA NA (or SHORT E), for the KHA-
TEPH-PATHACH (or SHORT A), of ADONAI.
Further, because the two first points attached to the
Divine name occur in a very great proportion of
Hebrew proper-names, as JEHONATHAN, JE-
HOSHAPHAT'; in which it is universally admitted
that the syllables JEHO represent the peculiar name
of THE DEITY, and that the names themselves are
properly translated by us JEHOVAH - HATH -
GIVEN, JEHOVAH - HATH - JUDGED.   And,
lastly, because the signification attributed by the
Almighty to the name יהוה leads to the punctuation found in the Masoretic text, and the pronunciation JEHOVAH.   "And Moses said unto God,
Behold, when I am come unto the children of Israel,
and shall say unto them, The God of your fathers
hath sent me unto you ; and they shall say to me,
WHAT IS HIS NAME ? what shall I say unto
them ?   And God said unto Moses, EHEYÈH
ASHÈR EHEYÈH, I SHALL BE THAT I
SHALL BE, I MUST BE THAT I MUST BE ;
and He said, Thus shalt thou say unto the children

of Israel, EHEYÈH, I-(THAT)-MUST-BE, hath
sent me unto you. And God said moreover unto
Moses, Thus shalt thou say unto the children of
Israel, יְהֹוָה, JEHOVAH, HE-(THAT)-MUST-BE,
the God of your fathers, the God of Abraham, the
God of Isaac, and the God of Jacob, hath sent me
unto you : this is MY NAME for ever, and this is
MY MEMORIAL unto all generations."* Now, the
future of the verb הָיָה, HAYAH, TO BE, in the
intensive form, and pointed as a proper-name, will
give the punctuation יְהֹוֶה, and the signification
HE-(THAT)-SHALL-BE, HE - (THAT) - MUST -
BE. For the final letter of this verb, the H, will
not be doubled (as in other words in the Piel future),
but the duplication will be transferred to the pre-
ceding Vau, and the form will be יְהוֶּה, JE-
HOVEH; and this future, by the change of
SEGOL into KAMETS, as the sign of the proper-
name,† will become יְהֹוָה, JEHOVAH. From
JEHOVAH we have the contracted forms יְהוֹ,
JEHO, יְ, JO, and יָהּ, JAH ;‡ the last being written
by the Greeks (with their silent S) IAS, and by the
Latins IA, the pronunciation in both cases being YA.
JAHU, YAHU, (יָהוּ), is compounded of יָהּ, and

* Exod. iii. 14, 15.   † Second Rule.   ‡ Psa. lxviii. 4.

הוּא; and is used at the end of a proper-name, to give emphasis to the appellation: as, אֵלִיָה, ELIJAH, ELIYAH, MY-GOD-IS-JEHOVAH; אֵלִיָהוּ, ELIJAHU, JEHOVAH-HE-IS-MY-GOD. And from the inquiry of Moses, "When they shall say unto me, What is His name, what shall I answer them?" and from a subsequent passage in Exodus,* "By my name JEHOVAH was I not known to them," it has been supposed that the INCOM-MUNICABLE NAME was first assumed by the Almighty when He spoke to Moses from the burning bush. But the supposition is perfectly incompatible with the fact, that the appellation enters into the composition of the names of persons existing long before the times of Moses. Thus, JUDAH, as we have seen, signifies JEHOVAH-WILL-I-CONFESS, and is so interpreted by Leah; and JOSEPH, the name of Rachel's eldest son, is JEHOVAH-HATH-ADDED, JEHOVAH-WILL-SURELY-ADD. She called his name JOSEPH, יְהוֹדוֹסִיף, JEHO-HOSIPH, יְהוֹדוֹסֵף, JEHO - HOSEPH, יְהוֹסֵף, JEHOSEPH,† יוֹסֵף, JOSEPH; "for she said, Jehovah will add to me another son." ‡   So

---

* Chap. vi. ver. 3.   † Psa. lxxxi. 5 (6).
‡ Gen. xxx. 24. Joseph. Antiq. lib. i. cap. xix. 8.

JOCHEBED is יְהוֹכָבֶד, JEHO-CHABED, JE-
HOVAH-HATH-PRESSED-SORE, THE-HAND-
OF-JEHOVAH-IS-HEAVY; and the name was, no
doubt, imposed by the parents of the mother of
Moses on their child in the days when the kings of
Egypt made the lives of the Israelites bitter with
hard bondage. Moses, then, can only be understood
as asking whether the Hebrews should still continue
to address the God of their fathers by His ancient
name, or whether the Almighty would at that time
reveal Himself to them by some other appellation,
or some addition to the name JEHOVAH. In
answer to the inquiry, God expounds the name; and
shows that it is proper to Himself alone, INCOM-
MUNICABLE, and incapable of application to any
other. All other beings may or may not be, for
their existence depends on the Creator; of Him only
can it be truly predicated, HE MUST BE. And
hence we may, perhaps, interpret the more difficult
text, " By my name JEHOVAH was I not known
to them;" that is, was I not comprehended by them.
For he is said in Scripture to be ignorant of that
which He does not fully understand. " And this
saying* was hid from them, neither knew they the

* Luke xviii. 34.

things that were spoken :" " For as yet they knew not
the Scripture, that He must rise from the dead."*
In both cases the disciples knew the words, but lacked
the comprehension of them.   And so it must ever
be with the Divine name JEHOVAH.   We may be
capable of analyzing it; and, interpreting it by the
rules of grammar, we may say that it signifies HE-
THAT-MUST-BE: but neither man nor angel can
go further; for the name involves the knowledge of
the mode of the Divine existence, comprehensible
by God alone: I-MUST-BE, is the utmost DEITY
can reveal; HE-MUST-BE, all that man can com-
prehend, concerning it.   And the patriarchs, thus
believing and worshipping, received from God the
end of their faith, even the salvation of their souls.
CHRIST was with this church as He was afterwards
with the church in the wilderness; THE LAMB
SLAIN FROM THE FOUNDATION OF THE
WORLD was with the WHOLE - BURNT -
OFFERING,† and through that sacrifice, as the
sacramental mean, was made unto them wisdom,
and justification, and sanctification, and redemption;
they were made sons of God by adoption; they

* John xx. 9.
† Job i. 5; xlii. 8. Numb. xxiii. 1, 14, 29, 30.

walked religiously in good works; * and they died in sure and certain hope of the RESURRECTION UNTO LIFE, † promised by the Almighty from the beginning of the world. ‡

*   *   *   *

THE TRADITION OF THE RABBINS makes the ÆNEAS of the Roman story an Idumean; and the inhabitants of the East insist that JOB was a descendant of Isaac's eldest son. JOB was perfect and upright, one that feared God and eschewed evil; and the piety and righteousness of ÆNEAS are prominent features of the Roman legend: " PIUS ÆNEAS :" "Insignis PIETATE vir :" " Rex, QUO JUSTIOR ALTER, nec pietate fuit, nec bello major et armis." Job worshipped God § by His name JEHOVAH, and the appellation ÆNEAS bears testimony to the religion of the father who imposed it on his son: עין־יה, AYIN-I-JAH; עיניה, ENIJAH; ‖ JEHOVAH-(IS)-MY-FOUNTAIN. " Thy mercy, O JEHOVAH, is in

* Gen. xxxix. 9. Job xxix. 11–17.

† Job xiv. 12, 14, 15. Psa. xlix. 14, 15. Acts xxiii. 6; xxiv. 15. Heb. xi. 19, 35.

‡ Luke i. 69, 70. Heb. ii. 14. Jude 6, 14.

§ Job i. 21.

‖ ENIYAH.

the heavens; * Thy faithfulness reacheth unto the
clouds: with Thee is the fountain of life." That
in flying to Italy, ÆNEAS was χρηματισθεις,† is
expressly asserted by the legend. "The reason
(writes Dionysius),‡ why the Trojan fleet sailed no
further into Europe, is to be attributed to the
oracles, and to the will of heaven, many ways revealed to them." In particular, the ship in which
Æneas sailed is said to have been built for him by
MERCURIUS, also called HERMES, the messen-
ger of the gods. Now, in Jewish phraseology, even
the unanimated agencies of nature are denominated
ANGELS or MESSENGERS of Jehovah, when
employed in the execution of the decrees of God.
"He § maketh the winds His angels, and His
ministers the fiery flame:" and so the tradition of
the Jews recognizes the lightning of heaven as the
ANGEL OF JEHOVAH by whom the host of
Sennacherib the Assyrian was destroyed. The story
places the arrival of Æneas in Italy, and the
building of the Laurentine Troy, three hundred
and thirty-three years prior to the date commonly
assigned to the foundation of Rome, or in the year

* Psa. xxxvi. 5, 9.   † Matt. 11. 22.
‡ Lib. i. c. 55.   § Psa. civ. 4.

before Christ one thousand and eighty-six. Saul, according to the Biblical chronology, ascended the throne of Israel in the year one thousand and ninety-five before Christ; and the Edomites were smitten by him in the earlier part of his reign. The utter destruction of the Amalekites by Saul must be placed some years after his victory over the Idu-means,* according to our Bible, about the year before Christ one thousand and seventy-nine. If, then, we can conceive an Idumean Æneas flying from Edom to escape the wrath of God, to avoid a destruction similar to that soon to be poured out on Amalek, and then on Edom, he might well, using the language of the Hebrews, declare himself impelled to flight by an angel of God, MERCURY or HERMES. For in the Hebrew (more properly, in the mouth of an Edomite, the Phœnician) tongue, MERĔC-UR (מְרָד־אוּר), by contraction † MERCUR, would signify FEAR-OF-FIRE; and חֵרֶם־אֵשׁ, KHEREM - ESH, contracted into KHERMESH, KHERMES, HERMES,‡ is the DOOM-OF-FIRE, the CURSE-OF-EXTERMINATION, pronounced by the Almighty against those sinners the Ama-

---

* 1 Sam. xiv. 47, 48; xv. 1, 15, 18.
† Rule Nine, p. 71.   ‡ Rule Eight, p. 70.

lekites, and by virtue of which men and beasts were to be put to the sword, and the cities, and all things found therein, utterly destroyed by fire.

But the tradition preserved by Varro assigns another angel to Æneas for a guide. " Ex* quo de Troja est egressus Æneas, Veneris ille per diem quotidie stellam vidit, donec ad agrum Laurentem veniret; in quo eam non vidit ulterius: qua re et terras cognovit esse fatales." If for TROJA, in this passage, we substitute EDOM, and for STELLA VENERIS, STAR OF JEHOVAH, we behold Æneas brought to Italy by the 'leading of a star,' even as the wise men of the East, long ages after-wards, followed a like guide, "till it came and stood still over where the young child was." And this tradition, grossly perverted, appears in other writers of the Roman story, who cause Æneas to recognise the TERRÆ FATALES, the land assigned him for his dwelling-place, by the ap-pearance of a WHITE SOW. "A SOW† beneath an oak shall lie along; ALL WHITE herself, and WHITE her thirty young. When thirty rolling years have run their race, thy son, Ascanius, on

---

* Servius on Æn. i. 382; ii. 801.

† Æn. viii. 61 (Dryden's translation).

this empty space, shall build a royal town of lasting fame; which from this omen shall receive its name." PORCA ALBA, translated from the Latin of Virgil into our own tongue, must certainly be rendered by the words WHITE SOW; but in the Phœnician spoken, as we assume, by Æneas the Edomite, these words would have a very different signification.   In that language, POREK, with the emphatic ה, and by contraction פֻּרְקָה, PORĔKA, PORCA, joined with עַל, AL, and בָּא, BA, PORCA-AL-BA, must be rendered, THE - RESCUER - OVERHEAD - GOING; and the WHITE SOW becomes identical with the GUIDING STAR of Varro.   Lycophron * changes the colour of this sow to BLACK, and calls her Συς Κελαινη; which appellation, however, contains the same idea, and refers itself to the same tradition: for PORCA NIGRA (פֻּרְקָה נִגְרָה) will signify THE-RESCUER-THE-DRAWER-OUT; THE-RESCUER-BY-DRAWING-OUT.

And here we stand on holy ground.   The Roman story takes its commencement in a marvel; a miracle worthy the long series of prophecy in the accomplishment of which Æneas was to act so great a part.   By the professors of that Rationalism (falsely so called),

* Cassan. ver. 1256.

which regards with equal eye the miracles of Moses,
and the marvels of modern magic, the tradition
will be scoffed at, and rejected : to the disciples
of a wiser creed we may say (with the Apostle),
That God is not the God of the Jew only, but of
the Gentile also; and (with the Evangelist), That he
was worthy for whom the Almighty should do this.
Perhaps it is possible to carry the tradition one step
higher; and, from God's doings with the patriarchs
of old, derive additional interest to the tale. "It
came to pass,* when God destroyed the cities of the
plain, that God remembered Abraham; and (by the
guidance of His angels) sent Lot out of the midst of
the overthrow, when He overthrew the cities in the
which Lot dwelt." And so, when the indignation of
the Lord was to be poured out on Edom, may not
the faith and the works of another of His servants
have come up in memorial before God; and may not
the Almighty, by the leading of His star, have
drawn this very ÆNEAS out of Idumea in remem-
brance, and as a descendant, of the PATRIARCH
JOB? Certain it is that the author (whoever he
was), of the ORIGO GENTIS ROMANÆ has connected the name of the perfect man of Uz with the

* Gen. xix. 29.

history of Rome. Speaking of the successor of
Æneas, he says, " Latini Ascanium, OB INSIG-
NEM VIRTUTEM, non solum Jove ortum credi-
derunt; sed etiam, per diminutionem, declinato
paululum nomine primo, JOBUM, dein postea
Iulum appellarunt." *

' Go,† hide thyself in Italy: there will I make of
thee a mighty people,' was, then, the voice of
Heaven; and Æneas the Idumean, his aged father,
and a few followers, pass to the coast of the Great
Sea: they take ship at Joppa;‡ and, in a single vessel,
along the shores of Africa they bend their course.

Virgil had, perhaps, some authority for making the
Tyrian Dido contemporary with Æneas; and it is
possible that these fugitive Edomites may have been
saved from shipwreck, and hospitably entertained by
this great queen. Her amour with Æneas may well
be treated as the mere invention of the poet; particularly as history has assigned another and a nobler
cause for Dido's death by her own hand. It is said,
indeed, that the foundation of Carthage did not pre-
cede that of Rome by more than seventy years; but
this is quite consistent with the account which makes
Queen Dido the builder of a much older place,

* Aur. Victor, p. 18, (Delph. edit.)　　† 1 Kin. xvii. 3.
‡ Jonah i. 3.

called BURSA. But, however the fact may be, the argument we have in hand will be greatly assisted and supported by an examination and analysis of the proper-names found in the history of the earliest Carthaginians, as commonly related; and (assuming, for the present, that the PUNIC VERSES OF PLAUTUS contain a language identical almost with the Hebrew of the Kings of Israel), we shall have little difficulty in determining the derivation of these names. DIDO, or DIDON, (דִּידֹה, or דִּידֹון), then, is deducible from the root דוד, and will signify BELOVED-ONE; ELISSA,* is a compound of אֵל־אִשָּׁה, EL-ISHSHA, HERO-WOMAN, HERO-INE; ANNA, is the Hebrew KHANNAH,† MERCY; BURSA, is a contraction of בִּירָה־אִשָּׁה, BIRA-ISHSHA, BIRISSA, BIRSA, WOMAN'S-CITADEL; and CARTHAGE of קִרְיַת־הַגּוֹא, KERETH-HAGGO, KARTHHAGGO, KART-HAGO, CENTRAL (OR MIDDLEMOST) CITY. Following the history of the Carthaginians to the times of Hannibal, we may say that the name of Rome's great enemy contains the cry uttered by the priests of Baal, in the presence of Elijah and the Israelites, at Carmel: עֲנֵה־בַּעַל, ANNE-BAAL, ANNIBAL, O-BAAL-ANSWER. The appella-

---

* Rule Seven, p. 70.   † Rule Eight, p. 70.

tion would seem to refer us to the famous oath. HAMILCAR is a compound of הַמֶּלֶךְכַּר, HAM-MELEKCAR, HAMMILCAR, PASTURE-(or, COUNTRY)-KING, equivalent, perhaps, to the Latin REGULUS.

Sailing from Carthage, Æneas and his companions at length attain the country given to them by the prophecy of Isaac; and thereupon (in token that they hail it as their appointed rest), they burn their ship.[*] They obtain a grant of land from some petty king of the aborigines, whereon they build a little town, and (repeating the cry with which they touched the shore) they name it תְּרֹדָיָה, TERO-JAH, TROJAH, TROJA,[†] SHOUT-(TO)-JEHOVAH. They call themselves LATINIM, and the country they inhabit לָמְיֹן, LATJON, LATLAND, DWEL-LING-PLACE-OF-THE-LAT. The name LA-TINIM is deducible from לוּט, TO VEIL, TO HIDE: if we derive the word from the participle present of this verb, it will signify HIDING-ONES; if from the past participle (with a forma-tive kamets [‡]), it means HIDDEN-ONES. The singular of this word is לָמְנִי, LATENI, LATINI,

* Dion. i. c. 72.   † Serv. Æ. i. 6; vii. 158. Liv. i. c. 1.
‡ Rule Two, p. 65.

the syllable 'נ, NI, (a portion of the pronoun אָנִי,
ANI, I), being postfixed to it. In the Biblical
Hebrew the possessive case (if it may so be called),
of this pronoun is formed by suffixing to the noun
the letter I, and its objective by postfixing to the
verb the syllable NI, preceded by the vowel-of-
junction, or punctum-glutationis; which last may
be A, E, or I. Thus, from EDOM the Hebrews
form the nomen gentile EDOM-I, (OF-EDOM-I),
AN EDOMITE. But this rule is not always observed; for, in the formation of the proper-names,
we find the letter YOD used to denote both the
possessive and objective forms of ANI. So SALA-
THIEL * is שְׁאַלְתִּיאֵל.† With the Latins, however,
the syllable NI appears most frequently as a suffix
in the formation of the name: and from LAT they
form LATINI, A LATIN; from TROJA, TRO-
JANI, A TROJAN.

That these fugitive Idumeans designated themselves HIDERS, or HIDDEN-ONES, by Divine
command, appears to be distinctly asserted by themselves, and, considered as imposed upon them by
God's direction, the name (like many of the Hebrew
proper-names) becomes prophetic; and describes a

* Page 62.   † Psa. lxx. 1.

people whose origin (at the first well known), would become veiled and hidden, to all except the prophets of the Lord. The universal opinion of the ancients traces the name LATIUM to the act of hiding: it was, they say, the LURKING-PLACE of SATURN, called by some a god, by others, an ancient monarch of the country. That the last tradition is the true one, and that Saturn is the good king Æneas, may be evidenced by the name itself. It appears to occur in two forms: סָתוּר־אֲנִי, SATUR-ANI, SATURNI, SATURN, HIDDEN-(AM)-I; and סָתוּר־אֲנִי־יָה, SATUR-ANI-IA, SA-TURNIA, HIDDEN-(AM)-I-(BY)-JEHOVAH. SATURN is to be considered as an abbreviation of SATURNIA, just as Josephus * should seem to call him BARUCH, (emphatically) BLESSED, whom our Lord speaks of † by his full name, BARA-CHIAS, JEHOVAH - HATH - BLESSED - (ME). " King Saturn," writes Justin,‡ "is said to have been of so much mildness, that under him neither was any one a slave, nor had private property any ex-istence: but all things were enjoyed by all men in common, and without distinction; even as a patri-

* Bell. Jud. lib. iv. cap. v. 4.   † Matt. xxiii. 35.
‡ Lib. xliii. cap. 1.

mony belonging to them all." We have here a
crowned Job. The name SATURNIA expounds
the appellation LATINIM, and shews it to mean
HIDDEN-ONES.

We have next to consider Æneas and his Idumeans
as WORSHIPPERS OF JUPITER. The words of
God to Moses, " THIS is my name, and this is my
memorial, to all generations," might seem to contain
a command that nothing should be added to the
appellation JEHOVAH, nor anything diminished
from it. The sequel of the history of the Exodus,
however, proves that this is not the meaning of the
text: " Fear ye not," said Moses to the people;
" stand still, and see the salvation of Jehovah:
JEHOVAH WILL FIGHT for you." " Then
sang Moses and the children of Israel to Jehovah,
saying, JEHOVAH IS A MAN OF WAR;" and
hence, I apprehend, arose the compellation JE-
HOVAH-SABAOTH, JEHOVAH - OF - HOSTS,
given by the Israelites to, and accepted of them by
God, in memory of the destruction of Pharoah and his
host. It is a condensation of the words JEHOVAH
IS A MAN OF WAR. Now, the peculiar relation
in which the Almighty stood to the Latins was that
of a deliverer from bondage; death or bands being

the alternatives offered by King David to the Edomites. They could not sing to Jehovah because He
had triumphed gloriously, because His right hand
had dashed in pieces the enemy; but they could say *
to the Almighty, "We are indeed thy servants,
O JEHOVAH; Thou hast LOOSED OUR
BONDS: we will offer Thee the sacrifice of thanksgiving, and will call upon the name of Jehovah."
Therefore, they endeavour to perpetuate the remem-
brance of the Divine mercy by the appellation
זְהוֹרִפֵּר, JEHO-PITTER, JOPITTER, JEHOVAH-
(THAT)-HATH-SET-FREE, JEHOVAH - THE-
ENFRANCHISER. The particulars of the worship offered to Jehovah by the patriarchs are easily
discoverable in the history of these Latins. Clean
beasts only could be laid upon His altar, which,
from the name, אֶל־טוּר, EL-TUR, ALTAR,†
GOD'S-ROCK, appears to have been formed of
unhewn stones.‡ The victim was consumed by fire,
whence the term, אוּרָיָ, URA, אָרָה, ARA, THE-
BURNER. And the altar was placed before an
OAK, thus rendered sacred.§ As with the patri-

* Psa. cxvi. 16.　† Second Rule, p. 65.　‡ Deut. xxvii. 5.
§ Deut. xiii. 18; xviii. 1 (Sept. Trans.). Josh. xxiv. 26. Isa.
i. 29. Liv. i. 10.

archs,* so with the oldest Latins, there was no
distinct priesthood: no traces of the worship of any
false deity are discoverable in their history; and
when their descendants forgat God their Saviour,
and were given up to strange delusions, to believe
a lie, and to the worship of all the abominations of
the heathen, the supremacy of Jupiter (degraded
from the Creator of all things, into the son of
his own creature,† Saturn or Æneas) was yet admitted and acknowledged. "Magnis de rebus dicere
exordiens, a JOVE incipiendum: quem unum
omnium deorum et hominum regem esse, omnes,
indocti doctique, consentiunt," writes Cicero.‡

In connexion with the worship of JUPITER, we
may consider the SATURNALIA in the light of
the greatest solemnity of the oldest Latins; instituted
(as its name and its observances testify), by ÆNEAS,
SATURNI, or the HIDDEN-ONE, in honour
of the Almighty, JEHOVAH-THE-ENFRAN-
CHISER, the God who had delivered the Latins
from the bonds prepared for them in Edom. The
name of this festival in Phœnician is סְטוּרְנִי־אֶל־יָה,
SATURNI-EL-IA, סְטְרְנִילְיָה, SATURNILIA; and as

* Gen. xiv. 18.   † Rom. i. 25.
‡ De Re. Pub. i. 37, (edit. Heinrich).

a noun, סַטְרְנַלְיָה, SATURNAL-IA, SATURNALIA, SATURNI-(or SATURN)-TO-JEHOVAH. The appellation is compounded of the names of the Deity in whose honour the festival was instituted, and of Æneas, by whom the observance of it was enjoined. The Saturnalia were instituted, say certain of the Romans, long before the foundation of Rome, in commemoration of the freedom and equality which prevailed on earth in the golden reign of Saturn; whilst others assert, that Janus first instituted the festival, in gratitude to Saturn, from whom he had learned agriculture. We shall see, hereafter, that Saturn and JANUS are the same person; JANUS being the DEIFIED SATURNI, or ÆNEAS. The celebration, we are told, was remarkable for the liberty which universally prevailed. In after-times, slaves (in the days of Saturn, servants), were allowed to speak with freedom upon every subject; friends made presents one to another; all animosity ceased; no criminals were executed; schools were shut; war was never declared; but all was mirth, and (with the Romans only) riot, and debauchery. The observance of the feast in the days of Æneas was, doubtless, in the spirit of that piety which called it into being; it answered to the Passover of the Jews,

when divested of the prophetic character; and by it
the Latins would make confession that, but for
the mighty hand of JEHOVAH* their God, bring-
ing them out of Edom, they had been servants in the
land of their nativity. There were, of course,
various other occasions on which the people came
together to worship, and to make merry before the
Lord; and these, as well as the Saturnalia, and
others having distinguishing names, appear to have
been comprehended under the general term CON-
SUALIA, כְּנֵסהוּאאֶליָה, CONES - HU - EL - IA,
כְּנֵסוּאֶליָה, CONSUELIA; as a noun, CONSUALIA,
A-GATHERING-(IS)-IT-TO-JEHOVAH. Thus,
the festival celebrated by Romulus when the Sabine
virgins were carried off, is said by some† to have
been held in honour of CONSUS, by others of
NEPTUNUS. The last word seems to be the
Phœnician נְפָתְהוּן, NE-PETHE-UN, NEPTUN,
A DILATING (or EXPANDING), to wit, of the
heart; a day of feasting and joy; of sending portions
one to another, and gifts to the poor.‡ It was,
probably, the feast of the SATURNALIA, or

---

* Deut. v. 15.

† Liv. i. cap. 9. Cic. De R. P. i. p. 56. Dion. ii. c. 30, 31.
Plut. Rom. xiv.   ‡ Esth. ix. 22.

PALILIA. In later times, the Romans appear to
have added the termination ALIA to the names of
various festivals (as, for instance, the MATRA-
LIA, clearly of foreign origin), without having
the slightest suspicion of its true and primitive
meaning.

* * * *

TROY being built, and the worship of God
established, the names of the different people by
whom Æneas and his Edomites were surrounded
fall next under our consideration: and these, I
should say, were comprehended by these Idumeans
under two grand divisions, the SABINES, and the
ETRUSCANS; the first appellation including all
but the Tuscans. SABINI, SABINIM, סבני, סבבים
from סבב SABAB, TO SURROUND, would mean
NEIGHBOURS; and portions of these SABINES
would, in process of time, receive distinctive appellations: as, שָׁמֶן־אִישׁ, SHAMEN-ISH, SHAMNIS,
SAMNIS, ROBUST-MAN, SAMNITE; שְׁבָלִים,
SOBELIM, שָׁבְלִים, SABELLIM, POURERS -
OVER, SABELLIANS, the people who afterwards overran so large part of Italy. It is manifest that the Roman story contradicts itself in
making Titus Tatius the king of a whole nation;

he could be no more than the ruler of some small
Sabine town and state, little, if anything, superior
to the Rome of Romulus in power and importance.
With regard to the ETRUSCANS, till some better
origin than that assigned them by Herodotus shall
be discovered, we must be content to call them
Mæonians, deriving their Grecian appellation, TYR-
RHENIANS, from the Tyrrhenus who led them
into Italy, and speaking a tongue Greek in its
original, but completely corrupted, and almost
swallowed up in the language of the Umbrians,
amongst whom they dwelt. The name TUSCAN
would seem to be of Phœnician origin, and would,
therefore, have been given to them by the Latins.
טוּרִאִישׁ, TUR-ISH, TURISK,* TURSK, (whence
the corruptions TURSICI, TUSCI, ETRUSCI),
WALL-MAN; an appellation well descriptive of
a people dwelling in towers, castles, and walled
cities, and as opposed to the SABINIM, who lived
in villages and towns destitute of walls.† And may
not the name RASENA, given to this people (in a
single passage only) by Dionysius, be Phœnician also;
and, like the PERSA of the Latins, referrible to their
horsemanship? "Persis," writes Bochart,‡ "nomen

* Rule Eight, p. 70.   † Plut. Rom. 16.   ‡ Phalg. iv. 10.

fuit ab equitatu, quo maxime valebant; equitare a teneris edocti." According to this derivation, PERSA, PERSIAN, will be of Phœnician origin; פָּרְשָׁה, PARASA, פְּרָשָׁה, PERASA, פָּרְשָׁה, PERSA, HORSEMAN: and so from רֶסֶן, RESEN, A BRIDLE, may come רְסָנָה, רָסְנָה, RASENA, A-BRIDLER, A-MAN-OF-THE-BRIDLE. Horses and horsemen, chariots and charioteers, fill a large space in the pictorial representations found on the vases and other monuments of Etruscan antiquity which have been preserved to us; and, according to Livy,* (perhaps, also, Tacitus,†) the Romans borrowed their horse-races from this very people. Even the name Τυρρηνος may be only another form of TURISH: מוּרְאָנשׁ, TURENOS, WALL-MAN.

●   ●   ●   ●

ÆNEAS, we are told, obtained in marriage the daughter of the king by whom, on his arrival in Italy, he had been hospitably received and entertained. A similar honour subsequently attended another flying Edomite. "When David was in Edom,‡ Hadad fled, he and certain of his father's servants with him, to go into Egypt: and they came

---

* Lib. i. c. 85.   † Annal. xiv. 21.
‡ 1 Kings xi. 17.

to Pharaoh king of Egypt, who gave him an house, and appointed him victuals, and gave him land: and Hadad found great favour in the sight of Pharaoh, so that he gave him to wife the sister of his own wife." This Hadad was 'of the king's seed in Edom;' and the Roman story makes Æneas, also, of royal extraction. The name LAVINIA must, being Phœnician, have been given by Æneas to his wife: לוהדאניריה, LAVA-ANI-IA, LAVINI-IA, LAVINIA, JEHOVAH-HATH-ADHERED-TO-ME. "Jehovah is on my side," says David; "I will not fear what man doeth unto me." Livy adds, that this event confirmed the hope of the new-comers that their wanderings would terminate in a permanent settlement in the land, a persuasion which seems to find expression in the name imposed by Æneas on the first child of the marriage: אֲשֵׁכְרָאֲנִי, ASACCENANI, ASCCENNI, ASCANI, * I-SHALL-DWELL-PEACEABLY. According to Dionysius, the first Silvius of the story was also the son of Æneas and Lavinia: שַׁלְוִי·שְׁלָרִי, SILVI, PEACEFUL-AND-PROSPEROUS-(AM)-I. An-other town is built, called LAVINIUM; but whether in honour of this Lavinia or not may be doubted:

* Second Rule, p. 65.

for the name LAVINIM, ADHERENTS, in the mouths of these godly or (so Dionysius calls them) 'god-like' men, would be equivalent to the term BRETHREN as used by the Christians of the Apostolic age; and thus LAVINION would receive its name, directly, from the LAVINES, as its builders.

And here the mortal acts of Æneas, so far as they affect the proper-names recorded by the story, appear to have their end. With his wars, the present argument, which confines itself to an examination of the legend as exhibited in these names, has no concern. If Æneas warred, we may well believe that he waged it in the spirit of Abraham, when he smote the kings, and brought again his brother Lot, and his goods, and the women also, and the people; and of Job, when he brake the jaws of the wicked, and plucked the spoil out of his teeth. He was buried, writes Livy, on the banks of the river Numicius; but, according to Dionysius, no man knew either the place of his sepulchre or the manner of his death; and by many he was supposed to have been translated to heaven without tasting death. After his removal from this earth he was called JUPITER INDIGES; and in the JANUS, יָהְדֵינוּ, JAH-NU,

JANU, OUR-JEHOVAH, of the Roman story, we
seem to recognize the DEIFIED ÆNEAS, one of
the DÆMONS, or DII MINORES, of the Latins.
The appellation OUR-JEHOVAH is a bold, and
(to us) irreverent expression; a character which, but
that they occur in Scripture, we should, perhaps,
attach to the words, "He calleth them gods unto
whom the word of God came." * The term OUR
may, however, so restrict and qualify the name as to
render it equivalent to A-GOD-UPON-EARTH, or,
A-GUARDIAN-ANGEL. The Rabbins derive the
Hebrew SHADDAI, THE ALMIGHTY, from
אֲשֶׁר־דַי, ASHER-DAI, WHO-(IS)-SUFFICIENCY;
and the Latin DEUS may have the like origin:
דַידוּא, DAI-HU, דֵידוּא, DE-HU, DEU, SUFFI-
CIENCY-(IS)-HE. Now the word DÆMON
(of which DEUS MINOR appears to be a later,
and exact, translation) would be formed from the
pluralis excellentiæ דַיִּם, DAIM, with the diminutive
ן, ON, DAIMON, DEMON; and, according to
this derivation, it would signify A MINOR GOD,
A MINOR SUFFICIENCY. "Deus," says
Festus, "dictus est, quod ei nihil desit." And so
ENOCH and ELIJAH, translated to heaven, and

* John x. 35.

made equal with the angels, and partakers of the Divine nature, became SUFFICIENCIES: but, forasmuch as their sufficiency was of God * alone, these Edomites seem to have denominated them (in common with the angels) DÆMONES, DII MINORES, MINOR GODS, MINOR SUFFICIENCIES. That the oldest Latins offered to Æneas, or their other dæmons, anything approaching to divine worship, there should seem to be no proof: in all probability they thought and spoke of them as the Jews do of their own Elijah; as of one who, though exalted to the highest heaven, is yet cognizant of the doings, and greatly interested in the welfare of his brethren upon earth. The SEMO SANCUS of the Latins appears to be the JUPITER INDIGES, or JANUS, in another form. For, if we read. the Hebrew שָׁנָה, SHANAH, with the hardened H,† or KH, then שְׁמוֹשָׁנְחוּ, SHEMO SHANĔKHU, SEMO SANCU, will signify HIS-NAME - HAVE - THEY - CHANGED, THE - DEITY-OF-THE-CHANGED-NAME.

Other circumstances indicating the identity of Æneas with Saturn, and of Saturn with Janus, may be detected amidst the corruptions and distortions

* 2 Cor. iii. 5.　　　　　† Rule Eight, p. 71.

of the true legend. Thus, Saturn is driven to Italy by the arms of Jupiter,* in the language of Scripture, by the sword of Jehovah and of David; Janus receives the fugitive Saturn, and makes him a sharer of his throne;† Janus coins money, one side of which he impresses with his own effigy, and the other with a representation of the ship which brought Saturn into Italy; and this ship appears also on the reverse of the Roman AS, which, from the earliest times, had on it the double-headed Janus.

* * * *

We may now proceed with the examination and analysis of the proper-names connected with the legendary history of Rome, in the order in which they are presented to us by the books of Livy.

Ascanius,‡ the son and successor of Æneas, built for himself a new town, called ALBA LONGA. " He transferred," writes Dionysius,§ " both the inhabitants of Lavinium and the other Latins, who were desirous of a better habitation, to his new-built city." The name ALBA LONGA, treated as belonging to the Latin of Livy, and translated into

---

* Ovid, Fast. lib. i. v. 235.   † Macrob. Saturnal. lib. i. c. 7.
‡ Liv. lib. i. cap. 3.   § Lib. i. cap. 56.

our own tongue, would be equivalent to LONG
WHITE-TOWN. The appellation ALBA is referred by the ancients to the omen of the WHITE
SOW,* already noticed; but, if this animal were,
in reality, the star which led Æneas into Italy, or if,
as Lycophron has it, the sow was black, some other
reason for the name ALBA must be discoverable.
The city, according to Livy, was called LONGA
from its situation, being extended on the ridge of a
hill. With the assistance of Strabo, we shall be
able to refer the words ALBA LONGA to the
Phœnician, the language of Æneas and his followers.
ALBA was seated in the middle of the dominions
of its founder,† and it was the political centre of
the Latin confederacy.   Now, the 'middle,' or
'centre,' of anything, is in Hebrew called its 'heart;'
as, for example, the 'heart of the sea,' the 'heart
of heaven.'   "The depths were congealed in the
heart of the sea."‡   "And the mountain burned
with fire unto the midst (literally, the heart) of
heaven."§   Cities, with the Hebrews, are of the
feminine gender, and so הַלִּבָּה, HALLĬBA,
HALLBA,‖ ALBA, THE HEART, would be

* Serv. on Æn. i. v. 270.   † Strabo, lib. v.   ‡ Exod. xv. 8.
    § Deut. iv. 11.   ‖ Ninth Rule, p. 71.

one name of the city built by Ascanius, expressive
both of its locality, as placed in the centre of his
kingdom, and of its political position, as the leader
of the confederated Latins. In Second Samuel *
we find a place called LO-DEBAR,† WITHOUT-
PESTILENCE; so named, no doubt, from its salu-
brity; and if to the particle LO, WITHOUT, we
subjoin a word of similar meaning with DEBAR,
we obtain the appellation לֹא־נֶגַע, LO-NĔGA,
LONGA, WITHOUT PLAGUE; and ALBA
LONGA, the city of Ascanius, is in reality ALBA
WITHOUT - PLAGUE, ALBA THE SALU -
BRIOUS. And such has been the character of the
Alban Mount, and the adjacent country, even to the
present day.

The transference of the supreme government of
the Latins to the city of the Mons Albanus carried
with it the great altar of the Latin Jupiter; thence-
forward called לְמִי־הַר, LATI-HAR, JUPITER
LATIAR, JUPITER OF THE LATIAN
MOUNT.

On the death of Ascanius, Sylvius, his son, (according to Dionysius, his brother), ascended the
throne. He was, says Livy (innocently enough),

* Chap. xvii. 27.   † Second Rule, p. 5.

"casu quodam in silvis natus."* This Sylvius was
the father of Æneas Silvius, who begot Latinus
Sylvius; and with Latinus Sylvius originated certain
colonies called by the historian PRISCI LATINI.
The translation of these terms by the words
ANCIENT LATINS is contradictory of the story;
since both Lavinium and Alba itself would have a
prior and preferable title to the name. " PRIS-
CUS," writes Niebuhr, " was certainly the title
of a people; and has exactly the same form and
character with the national names, Tuscus, Cascus,
and Opscus;" and this historian treats the appellation as equivalent to PRISCI ET LATINI. But
to this word, also, a Phœnician derivation, perfectly
consistent with the origin of these colonies, may be
assigned. For, if from the Hebrew PARASH, TO
SEPARATE, we form the participial noun פָּרִישׁ,
PĔRISH, and (Rule Eight †) pronounce this word
with the hardened H, PĔRISKIM LATINIM,
PRISKIM LATINIM, PRISCI LATINI, will
mean SEPARATED LATINS; colonies separated,
as it were, from the womb of Alba, their common
mother. Livy does not call the earliest inhabitants
of Rome ' Prisci Romani,' but ' Veteres Romani;'‡

* Lib. i. cap. 3.   † Page 71.   ‡ Lib. i. cap. 33.

and the term PRISCUS, in the sense of separated, is, when applied to the first Tarquin, in entire accordance with his story. For the name TARQUINIUS PRISCUS would be then of Latin origin, assumed by this king on becoming a citizen of Rome; and it would signify TARQUINIAN SEPARATIST, SECEDER FROM TARQUINII. And Dionysius furnishes us with the reason why Lavinium was reckoned amongst these Prisci Latini. It was, he says,* re-peopled by the Albans, who sent back some of their own people from Alba to Lavinium, to live there.

*   *   *   *

Little can be made of the names of the kings from Sylvius to Romulus and Remus: the list, as Niebuhr asserts of it, seems to be a very late and clumsy fabrication. To one of them, however, Romulus Sylvius, a Phœnician origin may be attributed. רום־מול־הוא, ROM-MUL-HU, ROMULU, BE-RISEN-BEFORE-HIM, STAND-UP-BE-FORE-HIM. "Thou shalt rise up before the hoary head, and honour the face of the old man;"† and the veneration in which Job was held by his countrymen is asserted in the text, "The young men

* Lib. i. cap. 67.   † Lev. xix. 32.

saw me, and hid themselves: even the aged arose, and stood up."* Romulus Sylvius, thus translated, will therefore be SYLVIUS THE VENERATED. This name, however, though consisting of the same letters, is not, I imagine, identical with that of the founder of Rome. The last contains a word of very different signification.

* * * *

We have next to read the legend of Romulus and Remus in connection with the proper-names to which it has given birth; and from these names to discover how much of the tale belongs to the genuine and ancient tradition of the Romans. The story of RHEA SILVIA (רִיאָה), LOOKED-AT SILVIA, SIGHTLY SILVIA, appears to involve the expression of the vow attributed by the Scriptures to Jephthah the Gileadite. He, we are told, vowed a vow, by virtue of which his only daughter became the Lord's, and was devoted to perpetual virginity; employed (as it should seem), in the services of the tabernacle of God. "He did with her according to his vow which he had vowed, and she knew no man." And the irrevocable vow, the vow from which Jephthah could not 'go back,' was

* Job xxix. 8.

made by the words, "I will offer her up for a
(WHOLE)-BURNT-OFFERING." Not that this
daughter of Israel was to be put to death; for the
service was to be a reasonable service, the sacrifice
a living sacrifice, holy, and acceptable to God: but
(as the Jews rightly understand the nature of the
vow), she was, symbolically, to be made a holocaust,
the flesh whereof was wholly the Lord's, and no
part of it could be reserved by the worshipper for
himself. So Amulius causes Rhea Silvia to become
A VESTAL; and, as a consequence, the obligation
of perpetual chastity is laid upon her: she is
made אִשָּׁה עַל־אֵשׁ, ISHSHA-AL-ESH, אֵשֶׁת עַל־אִישׁ,
ESHETH-AL-ISH, אֵשֶׁת־אֵשׁ, ESTALIS * (in later
Latin, and with the V prefixed by the Romans to
many words derived to them from the Greeks),
VESTALIS; A-WOMAN-(LAID)-UPON-THE-
FIRE, (symbolically), A - FEMALE - BURNT -
SACRIFICE. The Romans, in the times of their
subsequent ignorance of God and of His service,
found in this name the goddess VESTA, and her
sacred fire: but as we discover no traces, prior to
the days of Numa, of any worship amongst the
Latins save that offered by them to their Jupiter,

* Rule Seven, p. 70.

this holy flame would be the fire of His altar, which, like that of the altar of burnt-offerings * in the tabernacle of the Jews, might be kept always burning, and be never suffered to go out. The author of Judges adds to his narrative, " And it was a custom in Israel ;" which words seem to have been misunderstood by the commentators, and they refer (I apprehend) to the vow of Jephthah and its consequences, not to the succeeding verse, and the yearly lamentations of the daughters of Israel for Jephthah's daughter. Now it is quite possible that the Latins, as descendants of Esau, might possess many customs and observances found also amongst the sons of Jacob, and deriving their existence from times more ancient than the other institutions of the Mosaic Dispensation; and the vow here recorded may have been one of them; a portion, perhaps, of the rites of the patriarchal religion, even as it existed in the days of Noah and his sons. It is certain that the law of the Levirate Nuptials was obligatory on the descendants of Abraham centuries before the Exodus of the Israelites from Egypt.†

The examination and analysis of the names attaching to the story of the exposure and preserva-

* Lev. vi. 13.　　　　　† Gen. xxxviii. 8.

tion of the twin brothers must be preceded by extracting from the writings of Dionysius the tale, as he had it * from the lost history of Fabius Pictor. " By the order of Amulius, some of the king's officers took the children in a cradle (or trough, σκαφη), and carried them to the river, designing to throw them into it. When they drew near, and perceived that the Tiber, swelled by continual rains, had exceeded its natural bed, and had overflowed the plains, they came down from the top of the Palatine Hill to that part of the water which lay nearest, (for they could advance no farther), and set down the cradle upon the flood, where it washed the foot of the hill. The cradle floated for some time: then, as the waters retired by degrees from the utmost verge, striking against a stone, it overturned and threw out the children, who lay crying and wallowing in the mud. Upon this, a she-wolf, that had just whelped, appeared; and, her teats being distended with milk, gave them her paps to suck, and with her tongue licked off the mud with which they were besmeared. In the meantime, some shepherds happened to be driving their flocks to pasture (for the place was now become passable),

* Diony. lib. i. cap. 79.

and one of them, SEEING THE WOLF THUS
CHERISHING THE CHILDREN, was, for some
time, struck dumb with astonishment and disbelief
of what he saw : then, going away, and GETTING
TOGETHER AS MANY OF THE SHEP-
HERDS AS HE COULD, he carried them to see
the sight themselves. When THESE, ALSO,
drew near, and saw the wolf cherishing the children
AS IF THEY HAD BEEN HER YOUNG-
ONES, and the children HANGING ON HER
AS ON THEIR MOTHER, they imagined they
saw SOMETHING SUPERNATURAL, and ad-
vanced together, hallooing, to terrify the creature.
The wolf, not much frightened at the approach of
the men, but as if she had been tame, gently with-
drew from the children, GREATLY DESPISING
the mob of shepherds. There was, not far off, a holy
place, covered with a thick wood, and a hollow
rock. When the wolf came to this place, she hid
herself. The grove is no longer in existence, but
the cave is contiguous to the Palatine buildings,
and is to be seen in the way that leads to the Circus;
and near it stands a temple in which a statue is
placed representing this incident: it is A WOLF
SUCKLING TWO CHILDREN : they are in

brass, and are of ancient workmanship. As soon as the wolf was gone, the shepherds took up the children, and were very desirous to bring them up; and an overseer of the king's swineherds, whose name was Faustulus, a man of humanity, having received them by general consent, carried them home to his wife. As they grew up, he gave one the name of ROMULUS, the other, that of REMUS. The life of the children was that of HERDSMEN. They lived by their own labour, and, generally, on the mountains, in cottages of one story, which they built with wood and reeds; of which, one, called THE COTTAGE OF ROMULUS, remains even to this day, in the corner as you turn from the Palatine Hill to the Circus. It is kept sacred by those to whom the care of it is committed, who add to it no ornaments to render it more venerable; but, if any part of it is injured, whether by tempest or lapse of time, they repair the damage, and are careful to restore it, as nearly as may be, to its former condition."

Now, whilst the existence of the brazen wolf, and the cottage of Romulus, attest the popular belief of the legend, as related by Fabius Pictor, so will the names attributed by the Romans to the

chief actors in the story carry it upwards to times
more ancient than the oldest of their historians,
and to the reach of testimony deriveable from a
language, the existence of which, as a component
portion of his mother-tongue, would never be sus-
pected by any Roman wishing to corrupt the tradition of the fathers of the city, or to produce a tale
till then unheard. Here, first, we meet with LU-
PERCA, a goddess who caused the she-wolf to
treat Romulus and Remus so kindly; and thus
named, say some, from LUPA and PARCO. By
the Hebrews the wolf was called ZEEB, and by
the Greeks LUKOS: LUP therefore would be the
domestic name of the animal, its appellative amongst
the aborigines of Latium. If, then, to LUP we
subjoin the feminine of the Hebrew פָּרַק, A
SNATCHER-AWAY, A DELIVERER,* we
form the name LUP-פִּרְקָה, LUPPIRKA, THE-
WOLF-THE-SHE-DELIVERER. Next, we have
another goddess, RUMINA, who presided over
infants whilst at the breast, and the FIG-TREE,
called FICUS RUMINALIS, under which the
suckling of Romulus and Remus by the she-wolf is
supposed to have taken place.† In the Hebrew,

---

* Lam. v. 8.　　　　　　　† Liv. lib. i. cap. 4.

I

רֵעַ־אׄמְנָה רֹעֶה אׄמְנָה, RO-OMENA ,רוּמְנָה, RUMENA,
will signify SHEPHERD-NOURISHER; and, if
to this word we add the Latin formative ALIS,
FICUS RUMINALIS will be the FIG-TREE
OF THE-SHEPHERD-SUCKLER (or NOU-
RISHER): but if we take the termination ALIS
to be Hebrew, and to represent the words עַל (AL)
and אִישׁ (ISH), then the whole name רוּמְנָה־עַל־אִישׁ,
רוּמִינָלִישׁ, RUMINALIS, added to FICUS, will give
the appellation THE FIG-TREE OF THE-SHEP-
HERD-SUCKLER-IN-THE-SIGHT-OF-MAN.
And the suckled shepherd must be the LUPERCUS
of the Romans, Rome's founder Romulus, before the
building of the city, and by his foster-father called
LUP-פֶּרֶק, LUP-PĔRĔC, LUPERC, WOLF-DELI-
VERED; and the LUPERCALIA, LUPERC-אֶל־יהֹ,
LUPERC-TO-JEHOVAH; a feast of praise and
thanksgiving dedicated by the shepherd king to God,
in memory of his preservation by the she-wolf. In
a preceding page, I have resolved the appellation
ROMULU into the Hebrew רוֹם־מוּל־הוּא, ROM-
MUL-HU, with the signification VENERATED;
but this name, though it might have been given by
the Roman people to their king, could never have
originated with Faustulus, or been borne by Romu-

lus during his shepherd life. A very different derivation may, perhaps, be assigned to the title of Rome's first king; and it may be treated as a compound of the words רֹעֶה מֻל רֹעֶ‏מֻל, ROMUL, or, with the emphatic הוא, ROMULU; A-SHEP-HERD-HERETOFORE, THE-QUONDAM-SHEPHERD. On the last supposition, the appellation must have been assumed by the king himself, who, like God's servant David, had been taken from the sheepfolds and from following the ewes great with young; and it will bear testimony both to the humility and magnanimity of its royal author, and to the certainty of the legend of the she-wolf. The grand objection to this derivation of the name arises from the fact, that in the small store of Hebrew we possess, MUL, (ANTE), is never used in respect of time, but has reference to place only. On the other hand, we have the word ETHMUL, with the signification HERETOFORE, and this would appear to be a compound of MUL and the particle ETH (אֶת‏מֻל); whence, perhaps, arises a strong presumption that MUL itself, divested of this prefix, might also possess the meaning belonging to the compound word. In either case, ROMULUS must, before the building of the city, have had some other designa-

I 2

tion; and his first name will, I imagine, be found in the appellation LUPERC. This name appears also in the word LUPERCAL, (Luperc-עַל), LUPERC'S-HEIGHT, designating either the whole Mons Palatinus, or that portion of it where the she-wolf came to the rescue of the sons of Rhea Silvia. REM, or REMU, (רְאֵם, or רָאֵם־הוּא), signifies in Hebrew, WILD-BULL, BUFFALO, an animal still inhabiting the country between Rome and Ostia.* The depths of the religious ignorance into which the once wise and understanding Romans fell may be estimated and evidenced by the treatment which the story of Romulus and Remus met with at their hands in after-times. For, from this source alone, they seem to have derived their divinities VESTA, LU-PERCA, RUMINA, and LUPERCUS; all of whom appear to be mere creations of philological speculation, employed in determining the derivations of the words VESTALIS, LUPERCAL, RUMINALIS, and LUPERCALIA. They became vain in their imaginations, and their foolish heart was darkened; they forgot the name of the God of Æneas; they lifted up their hands to strange gods; they provoked Jehovah to anger with their inven-

* Rome in the Nineteenth Century. Edin. 1820. Vol. iii. 413.

tions; and the plague of their perverted theology brake in upon them.

*　　*　　*　　*

ROMA. The name of the Eternal City, רוֹמָה, ROMAH, is pure Hebrew; a noun formed from רוּמָה, RUMAH, the feminine of the past participle of the verb רוּם, RUM, by the change of SHUREK (U) into KHOLEM (O); and it signifies THAT-HAS-BEEN-EXALTED. The use of the past participle in the formation of the word appears to express, not merely the position of the URBS SEP-TICOLLIS, but the persuasion of the founders of this DOMINA GENTIUM, that (in the words of Obadiah *), their city would "exalt herself as the eagle, and set her nest amongst the stars."

POMŒRIUM. When referred to the Hebrew, may be treated as a compound of פוֹ, PO, the enclitic מוֹ, MO, (after the form כְּמוֹ), עִיר, IR, and the formative יוֹן, ION: פוֹמוֹרְעִירִיוֹן, POMOIRION, POMŒ-RIUM, THE-HITHERTO-OF-THE-CITY.

REMURIA, רֵאמִרְיָאָה, REMU-RIA, will, in Hebrew, signify REMUS'-CHOICE; the hill, some miles below Rome, on the Tiber, where Remus wished the city to be built.

* Verse 4.

PALATIUM. The Hebrew פָּלַט, PALAT, ONE THAT ESCAPES, joined to the formative יוֹן, ION, will make the Mons Palatinus mean PLACE-OF-THE-PALAT, (OR REFUGEE). The hill would therefore be so called as the REFUGIUM and dwelling-place of Romulus and Remus, delivered from Amulius by the she-wolf, and nurtured by the shepherds; and hence would come the tale that Romulus made Rome an asylum for runaway slaves. That such would be received and entertained by him we may believe, for so had the sons of Jacob been commanded; but it does not follow that Romulus resorted to this expedient to increase the population of his city. "Thou shalt not deliver unto his master the servant which is escaped from his master unto thee; he shall dwell with thee in that place which he shall choose, in one of thy gates, where it liketh him best." *

CAPITOLIUM. In Hebrew, כַּפִּיתְלִיוֹן, CAPPI-TOL-ION, CAPITOLION, THE-PLACE-(WHEREAT)-TO-UPLIFT-THE-HAND; the place of worship and prayer, and of the 'lifting up of holy hands.'† Here, according to Livy, stood the oak (and, no doubt, the altar) sacred to Jupiter; and

* Deut. xxiii. 15.　　　　† 1 Tim. ii. 8.

in this holy mount, thence also called צַרְפֶּה־יָּה,
TSAR-PE-IAH, TARPEIA, ROCK-OF-THE-
MOUTH - OF - JEHOVAH, the devout Romans
awaited God's answers to their prayers. With the
Greeks and Romans, the Hebrew TSADDE, or TS,
is represented by S, or T, or Z; but they seem to
have been unable to enunciate this letter as pronounced by the Jews. Jerome, speaking of it,
says, "Zadde, quam nostræ aures penitus reformi-
dant."

COMITIUM. By the Romans of the Augustan
age derived from CON and ITUM; but in the
Hebrew קְמֵט־יוֹן, KOMET - ION, COMITION,
PLACE-OF-FETTERING, of TYING-HAND-
AND-FOOT. Here the assembled people gave
their assent to laws, and so put on themselves the
shackles of legal obligation.

REX. This word, referred to the Hebrew, will
be a compound of רָגַע, RAGA, TO STIR UP,
AGITATE, PUT INTO COMMOTION, and אִישׁ,
ISH, MAN; רְגִישׁ רְגָעאִישׁ, REGIS, REGS, REX.
The elective king of the Romans was the great
STIMULATOR, PROVOCATOR, of their TU-
MULTUS, or LEVY EN MASSE.

TRIBUS. The word TĔRIB, by contraction

TRIB, considered as a derivative from רָבָה,
RABAH, TO BE NUMEROUS, appears to be
analogous with the Latin MULTITUDO, and the
Greek ΠΛΗΘΟΣ; and to denote the aggregate of
the individuals, whether Ramnes, Titienses, or
Luceres, of which it was made up: תִּרְבֶּה, תִּרְבִּים,
TRIBBEH, TRIBBIM, TRIBE, TRIBES.

RAMNES. TITIENSES. LUCERES. The
resolution of the names of the tribes into Hebrew,
converts them from nations into three distinct castes,
composed of the nobles, the husbandmen, and the
handicraftsmen. The obsolete ENESH, from which
the common Hebrew plural ANASHIM is formed,
will (the authority of Festus admitted) be found in
each of these appellations. Thus, רָם־אֱנָשׁ, RAM-
ENES,* (by contraction) RAMNES,† is, literally,
HIGH-FELLOW; and מִיט־אֱנָשׁ, TIT-ENES, TIT-
ENS, or, with Yod inserted, TITIENS, means SOIL-
MAN, MAN-OF-THE-SOIL, HUSBANDMAN.
The Hebrew ICCAR, DIGGER, PLOUGHMAN,
HUSBANDMAN, refers us to a root ACAR,
synonymous (as in the Arabic) with פָּרָה, CARAH,
TO DIG; and if to the participle of this verb we
prefix the particle לֹא, LO, (or the Latin NON), and

* Rule Seven, p. 70.　　　† Rule Nine, p. 71.

subjoin to it the word אִישׁ, ISH, MAN, we form the
appellation לֹא־אֹכֵר־אִישׁ, LO-OCER-IS, LOOCERIS,
LUCERIS, NON-DIGGING-MAN, HANDI-
CRAFTSMAN. If, as Festus asserts, the members
of the third tribe were also called LUCERENSES,
the word ENES, as found in RAMNES and
TITIENS, will enter into the composition of this
name, and LUCER-ENES, LUCERENS, will be
exactly equivalent to LUCERIS.

SENATOR. אֲשֶׁר־נָטֹר, ASHER-NATOR, שְׁנָטֹר,
SHENATOR, SENATOR,* WHO - IS - TO -
WATCH, WHO- IS-TO- GUARD; the senators
being peculiarly those to whom, as to guardians and
watchmen, the safety and welfare of the people were
committed.

PATER. "Patres certe ab honore appellati,"
writes Livy; and his notion of the origin of this
title, as borne by the Roman senators, may be cor-
rect, without giving the name the signification of
'father,' 'parent,' which, in the vocabulary of this
historian, appears to be the Greek Πατηρ, and to be
derived to the Latin directly from the language of the
Greeks. The Hebrew פָּטַר, PATER, signifies ONE
WHO IS RELIEVED FROM SERVICE, as in

* Rule Seven, p. 70.

FIRST CHRONICLES:* "And these are the singers, chief of the fathers of the Levites, who, remaining in the chambers, were PATURIM, FREE FROM (all other) SERVICE; for they were employed in that work (or service) day and night." And so the ROMAN SENATOR, engaged at all times in the Senate-house in his capacity of watchman for the welfare, and guardian of the lives and liberty of the people, was a PATER, or Pater-אִישׁ, PATERIS, PATRIS; one relieved from the military and all other services incumbent on the residue of the members of the state.

PATRICIUS. PLEBS. PLEBS, or PLEBIS, will, in Hebrew, be a compound of פֶּה־לֵב־אִישׁ, PĔ-LEB - IS, by contraction, PLEBIS, PLEBS, MOUTH-HEARTED-MAN, MOUTH-MINDED-MAN; one whose whole attention is taken up and engrossed by the care of providing for his daily subsistence. The name PATRIC, or PATRICI, should seem to be the opposite of PLEBS, and to be derived from the root TARAK, which occurs but once in the Hebrew of the Bible: פֶּה־טָרַח, PETEREKI, PATRIKI, A-FLINGER-AWAY-OF-THE-MOUTH; one relieved from the cares

* Chap. ix. 33.

incident to the task of making daily provision for his existence; one who, unlike the PLEBS, does not ' live from hand to mouth.'

PATRONUS. CLIENS. In many cases the Hebrew termination ON has the force of a diminutive; and so from ISH, A MAN, they denominate the pupilla of the eye ISHSHON AYIN, THE LITTLE MAN OF THE EYE. If, then, to the name PATER, considered as an appellative peculiar to the Senator of the Romans, we subjoin this formative ON, we obtain the name PATER-ON, by contraction PATRON, with the signification PATER MINOR, that is, MINOR SENATOR, MINOR WATCHMAN, MINOR GUARDIAN. And such was the relation in which the PATRO-NUS stood to his CLIENTS, as the guardian of their individual interests, and as contrasted with the SENATOR, to whose keeping the welfare of the whole body of the people was entrusted. The SENIORES and JUNIORES PATRUM are often placed in opposition by Livy; but (as Niebuhr remarks), in supposing all these PATRES to be senators, differing in temper according to their ages, both he and Dionysius must certainly have been mistaken. Thus, in Livy's narrative of the conduct

of L. Furius and C. Manlius, when accused, we read
that " circumeunt sordidati non Plebem magis quam
juniores Patrum;"* they canvassed not merely the
plebs, the populace, but such of the Patricians as
had clients amongst the plebs; such of the Patricians
as were also Patrons. For it is unnecessary to suppose
that every PATRICIAN was also A PATRON:
on the contrary, the privilege of receiving persons
into clientship is said, in the first instance, to have
been claimed by the Patricians of the Ramnes, to the
exclusion of the Patricians belonging to the other
tribes; and even amongst the Ramnes, there may
have been Patricians without a single client.

CLIENS. חִלְיָאנָשׁ, KILLE-ENES, KILLIENS,
KLIENS, will, in Hebrew, denote A SUPPLI-
CATOR OF ANOTHER, ONE WHO IM-
PLORES THE FAVOUR OF ANOTHER.

PALILIA. The foundation-day of Rome was
celebrated on the twenty-first of April, being (it is
said) the festival of PALES, the goddess of shepherds; but the term PALILIA, when referred to
the Hebrew, discloses a very different signification.
פְּלָאאִלְיָה, PALA-EL-IAH, PALILIA, HE-HATH-
DEDICATED - (THE CITY) - TO - JEHOVAH,

* Liv. lib. ii. cap. 54.

IT-IS-DEDICATED-TO-JEHOVAH. It should seem impossible to read the history of Romulus without perceiving that he acknowledged no god save the Jupiter of his fathers; and that Mars, Vesta, and the other divinities of the story, are the creations and fictions of the ignorance of later times. And may not this very name PALILIA have been the SECRET (or LESS KNOWN) NAME of Rome, perpaucis cognitum, neminique revelandum; and involving that of the Tutelaris Romæ Deus, by some believed to be Jupiter himself,[*] that is, IA?

QUIRIS. קִירָאִישׁ, KIR-IS, CITY-MAN, CITIZEN, literally, WALL-MAN, one living within the walls of the city, as opposed to those who dwelt in the open country. The Roman Q is said by Quintilian to have been obtained from the Greeks, and to be the KOPPA of their alphabet; but both these letters will best be referred directly to the Phœnician KOPH.

TALASSIUS.   TALASSIO.   TALASSUS. THALASSIUS. Plutarch seems to have preserved the true origin of this cry; and the uplifting of the bride, by which it was accompanied, will enable us to trace it to a Phœnician origin. It was, he

---

[*] Macrob. Saturnal, iii. 5.

says, the signal given by Romulus * for the commencement of the rape; and it is worthy of observation that Plutarch derived this version of the word
from a Carthaginian, Sextius Sylla, who, speaking
the Phœnician tongue, would recognize in it
a meaning lost to the Romans and the Greeks.
This nuptial cry should seem, then, to be a corruption of תֵּל־אִשָּׁה, TOL-ISHSHA, תָּלְשָׁה, TALISH-
SHA, TALISSA, LIFT-WOMAN.

FERETRIUS. פְּרֵעָאת־עִירִי, PARA-ETH-IRI,
PHERETHIRI, PHERETRI, JUPITER-(THAT)-
HATH-LED-ON-MY-CITY. " O God, when thou
wentest forth before thy people, when thou marchedst
out of the field of Edom, the earth trembled, and
the heavens dropped."†

STATOR. This epithet, if referred to the
Hebrew, may be derived from the obsolete מוט,
TUT, TO COLLECT, TO GATHER TOGE-
THER; אֲשֶׁר־טָט, ASHER-TAT, שָׁטָט, SHĔTAT,
STAT, JUPITER-STAT, JUPITER-THE-RAL-
LIER. " Ut Hostus cecidit, confestim Romana
inclinatur acies; fusaque est ad veterem portam
Palatii."‡

---

* Rom. xv.   † Psal. lxviii. 7. Jud. v. 4.
‡ Liv. i. 12.

TEMPLUM. תִּמְפְלֹח, TĔMIPHLON, תִּמְפְלֹח,
TĔMPĔLON, TEMPLON, A-SEPARATED-
PLACE, A-CONSECRATED-PLACE. The
temples dedicated by Romulus to Jupiter, as the
LEADER and RALLIER of the Romans, should
seem to have been altars of the nature of those
consecrated to the Almighty by Jacob and Moses.
"And Jacob built an altar and called the place
EL-BETH-EL; because there God appeared unto
him." "And Moses built an altar, and called the
name of it JEHOVAH-MY-BANNER."

SPOLIA OPIMA. Abraham, returning from
the slaughter of the kings, gives a tithe of the spoil
to Melchizedek, as the priest of the most high
God, in token that he owns his victory to be from
the Almighty; so the children of Judah offer to the
Lord of the spoil which they have taken of the
Ethiopians; and so, the Dictator Camillus * devotes
to Apollo a tenth part of the spoils of the Veientes.
Now the words SPOLIA OPIMA appear to con-
tain the Hebrew following: אֲשֶׁר פֹּלֵא יָה עוֹד־אֵימָה,
ASHER-POLE-IA-OPH-EMA, SE-POL-IA-OP-
IMA, SPOLIAOPIMA, WHAT-JEHOVAH-THE-
BRANDISHER-OF-TERROR-SEPARATES (or

* Liv. v. 21.

CONSECRATES). "And the terror of God (terror spread by God), was upon the cities that were round about them, and they did not pursue after the sons of Jacob."

QUIRINUS. קִירְעֵין, KIR-AYIN, קִירְעֵין, KI-REN, CITY-EYE, EYE-OF-THE-CITY. The epithet may be compared with the OCULUS MUNDI, or SUN, of the Romans.

NUMA POMPILIUS. Numa seems to be the Hebrew נְאֻם, with the emphatic ה. NEÜMA, NEUMA, NUMA, AN ORACLE; and Pompilius, פּוֹרְמְפִלָּהִי, PO-MEPILLEH-I, POMPILLI, HERE-(WAS)-MY-CONSECRATION, HERE-WAS-I-MADE-A-KING. POMPILI THE ORACULAR.

SACERDOS. סַכְּרִעֵד, SACER-ED, SACERD, LOCKER-UP-(OR KEEPER)-OF-THE-TESTI⸱MONY. In thirty-first Exodus,* the testimony denotes the commandments of God, written on two tables of stone.

DIALIS. דִּי־אֵל־אִישׁ, THE-ALMIGHTY'S-MAN; MAN-OF-JUPITER, called the (ALL)-SUFFICI-ENT-GOD.

FLAMEN. פְּלָא־אָמֵן, PALA-AMEN, פְּלָאמֵן, PELAMEN, PHLAMEN, CONSECRATED-IN-

* Verse 18.

PERPETUITY. It answers exactly to the SACERDOS ASSIDUUS of Livy.*

TARQUINIUS PRISCUS. LUCUMO. If the appellation PRISCUS be deriveable from the Hebrew,† and the names TARQUINIUS PRIS-CUS signify in reality TARQUINIAN SEPARA-TIST, SECEDER FROM TARQUINII, then LOCUMO, לא־קימאו, LOCOMO, לא־קימה, NOT-TO-RISE-ONE, NON-RISER, may be Hebrew also, an appellative given to the first Tarquin and other Etruscans by the Romans. "Anco regnante, LUCUMO,‡ vir impiger ac divitiis potens, Romam commigravit, cupidine maxime ac spe magni honoris, cujus adipiscendi Tarquiniis, nam ibi quoque pere-grina stirpa oriundus erat, facultas non fuerat." " Lucumo," says Niebuhr, § " is nowhere found in the Etruscan inscriptions, and the old philo-logians knew that it was no name."

ITALIA. This name, referred to the Hebrew (התלי־יה, HITTALLI-IA, HITTAL-IA, ITA-LIA), will mean MAYEST - THOU - BE - EX-ALTED - BY - JEHOVAH. The greatest uncer-tainty appears to exist respecting the locality and

---

* Lib. i. c. 20.   † Page 106.
‡ Liv. i. 34.   § Lect. on Rom. Hist.

K

extent of the most ancient Italy. Regarded as an appellation originally confined to Rome and its territory, it would explain many of the prophecies by which the utter destruction of the mystical Edom is foretold; and a direct reference to it would then be found in the name given by the Romans to their city.

＊　　　＊　　　＊　　　＊

The evidence of PROPHECY has next to be adduced in support of the TRADITION OF THE RABBINS, and in proof of the IDUMEAN ORIGIN of the ROMAN PEOPLE. Concerning the monster depicted in the thirteenth chapter of the Revelation of Saint John, Bishop Newton writes thus. "No doubt is to be made that this beast is designed to represent the Roman Empire; for, thus far, both ancients and moderns, papists and protestants, are agreed: the only controversy is, whether it be Rome Pagan or Christian, Imperial or Papal." Little less than the like agreement exists (as the Bishop also remarks), with regard to the dominion intended by the Fourth Beast of the prophecy of Daniel: " This fourth kingdom can be none other than the Roman Empire; and Calmet himself acknowledges that it is usually explained of the

Roman Empire." The prophecy of Saint John is, therefore, supplementary to that of Daniel, and from it we obtain much of the description of THE FOURTH KINGDOM UPON EARTH intentionally omitted by the Hebrew prophet; kept back, and reserved to be revealed in the fulness of time. The FOURTH BEAST, Daniel tells us, was "dreadful and terrible, and strong exceedingly; it had great iron teeth, and it had ten horns." Here the prophet stops. In other particulars, not noticed, this Beast was "diverse from all the Beasts that were before it." And for these diversities, and to complete the description of the Fourth Beast of Daniel, we must have recourse to the Revelation of Saint John. From his prophecy we learn that this Beast had "seven heads, and ten horns, and upon his horns ten crowns; that he was like unto a leopard; that his feet were as the feet of a bear, and his mouth as the mouth of a lion; that (like Esau) he was scarlet-coloured; and that upon his seven heads (representing seven hills) was seated a woman (or city), being that GREAT CITY which (when the vision was seen by the Apostle) reigned over all the kings (or kingdoms) of the earth." Of this Beast it is further written that " there was given

unto him a mouth speaking great things and blasphemies;" also, " that it was given unto him to
make war with the saints, and to overcome them;"
and, also, " that power was given him over all
kindreds, and tongues, and nations;" in the words of
Daniel, " he was to devour the whole earth, and
tread it down, and break it in pieces." The ten-
horned Beast of Daniel being, then, identical with
the ten-horned and seven-headed Beast of the
Apocalypse, and each of them representing the
Roman Empire in some stage of its existence, and
during its progress to perdition, the prophecy further
declares that the Beast has a numbered name, a
name which (using its component letters as numerals) may be measured, or exhibited, by letters,
amounting in the sum to six hundred and sixty-six.
"Here is wisdom. Let him that hath understanding
count the number (of the name) of the Beast: for it
is the number (of the name) of a man; and his
number (the number of his name) is SIX HUN-
DRED THREESCORE AND SIX." *" It is not,
therefore,* a vain and ridiculous attempt to search
into this mystery; but, on the contrary, it is recom-
mended to us upon the authority of an apostle: the

* Bishop Newton.

number only is specified; and from the number we must, as well as we can, collect the name." But the prophecy does not declare in what language this name is to be counted; whether in the Greek of Saint John, the Hebrew of Daniel, or the mother-tongue of the Beast himself; and hence, perhaps, we may collect that it will be found in all of them, and (for this should seem essential to the certainty of the interpretation), in no other language of the earth. From the Greek, the late Dr. Adam Clarke has produced the words 'Η ΛΑΤΙΝΗ ΒΑΣΙΛΕΙΑ, one, we may well believe, of the names intended by the prophecy. Let us now see how much further the method of interpretation suggested by this commentator may be carried by means of the Hebrew of Daniel, being also the mother-tongue of Esau, the father of the Edomites. And the Hebrew, thus applied, discloses to us the following names, or descriptions, of the APOCALYPTIC BEAST; all comprising the number 666.

ממשל הרומה:

THE ROMAN EMPIRE.

מלכות האדמי והלטני:
מלכות אדמי ולטיני:

THE KINGDOM OF THE EDOMITE, OR LATIN.

ממשל האדומים והלטנים:

ממשל אדומים ולטינים:

ממשל אדומיים ולטנים:

THE EMPIRE OF THE EDOMITES, OR LATINS.

הממלכות לאדמים:

THE KINGDOM OF THE EDOMITES.

מלכות ארום ואדמי בנו:

THE KINGDOM OF EDOM, AND OF THE EDOMITE, HIS SON.

ממלכת אדמי ואדום אביהו:

THE KINGDOM OF THE EDOMITE, AND OF HIS FATHER, EDOM.

הממלכה של אדום הוא היה אבי האדמים:

THE KINGDOM OF EDOM: HE WAS THE FATHER OF THE EDOMITES.

והממלכה לעשו הוא אבי אדמים:

THE KINGDOM OF ESAU: HE WAS THE FATHER OF THE EDOMITES.

ממלכה לעשו ואדום אבי אדמי:

THE KINGDOM OF ESAU, ALIAS EDOM, THE FATHER OF THE EDOMITE.

*   *   *   *

And in Italy, and on Rome, say the Rabbins, will the prophecies of the prophets against Esau, Edom, and the cities of Edom, be fulfilled. "The sword of the Lord is filled with blood: for the Lord hath

a sacrifice in Bozrah, and a great slaughter in the
land of Idumea. And the streams thereof shall be
turned into pitch, and the dust thereof into brim-
stone, and the land thereof shall become burning
pitch: it shall not be quenched night nor day; the
smoke thereof shall go up for ever and ever: from
generation to generation it shall lie waste; none
shall pass through it for ever and ever." "Who is
this that cometh from Edom, with dyed garments
from Bozrah? this that is glorious in his apparel,
travelling in the greatness of his strength? I that
speak in righteousness, mighty to save. I have
trodden the wine-press alone; and of the people
there was none with me: for I will tread them in
mine anger, and trample them in my fury; and
their blood shall be sprinkled upon my garments,
and I will stain all my raiment." "Whereas Edom
saith, We are impoverished, but we will return and
build the desolate places; thus saith the Lord of
Hosts: They shall build; but I will throw down:
and they shall call them THE BORDER OF
WICKEDNESS, and, The people against whom
the Lord hath indignation for ever." "And THE
BEAST opened his mouth in BLASPHEMY
AGAINST GOD; to blaspheme His name, and

His tabernacle, and Them that dwell in heaven."
"And the great winepress of the wrath of God was
trodden without the city, and blood came out of the
winepress, even unto the horse-bridles, by the space
of a thousand and six hundred furlongs." "And
there was a great earthquake, such as was not since
men were upon the earth so mighty an earthquake,
and so great; and the GREAT CITY was divided
into three parts; and the cities of the Gentiles fell;
and BABYLON THE GREAT came in remem-
brance before God, to give unto her the cup of the
wine of the fierceness of his wrath." "Her plagues
shall come in one day, death, and mourning, and
famine; and she shall be utterly burned with fire."
"And the kings of the earth shall lament for her,
when they shall see the smoke of her burning,
saying, What city was like unto this great city."
"With violence shall that great city Babylon be
thrown down, and shall be found no more at all."
"And the house of Jacob shall be a fire, and the
house of Joseph a flame, and the house of Esau for
stubble." "And saviours shall come up on Mount
Zion to judge the house of Esau; and the KING-
DOM SHALL BE THE LORD'S."*

* Rev. xix. 1, 2, 6.

APPENDIX.

THE INTERPRETATION ATTEMPTED OF THE PHŒNICIAN VERSES FOUND IN THE PŒNULUS OF PLAUTUS.

[WITH CORRECTIONS AND ADDITIONS.]

APPENDIX.

THE fifth act of the PŒNULUS opens with the appearance of THE CARTHAGINIAN in the public streets, in search of his stolen daughters; and its first scene consists of a soliloquy delivered by THE BILINGUIS, partly in the languages of his own countrymen, and partly in the Latin of his Roman audience. Of the SIXTEEN VERSES which constitute the PUNIC portion of this soliloquy, I treat the FIRST TEN as belonging to the PHŒNICIAN, or CANAANITISH, tongue: the remaining SIX, together with the shorter, non-Latin, speeches of HANNO and the NURSE, found in the two succeeding scenes of the same act, I refer to the LIBYC dialect of the soliloquist.

Amongst the host of scholars who have laboured at the elucidation of these verses, two only, BOCHART and GESENIUS, have produced anything approaching to an interpretation of them; and of their expositions it may here be sufficient to observe, that they are, for the most part, contradictory and subversive of each other; exhibiting little more than the discordant results of conjectural criticism, employed in the emendation of a text which (in the judgment of the critics), the mistakes of the copyists have rendered all but incurably defective, and irretrievably depraved. BOCHART, referring to the common text, as printed in his Phaleg, terms it, "Decem versus prout corrupte scribuntur in Plauti editionibus:" "Certum est," writes GESENIUS, "omniumque criticorum consensu approbatum, Plautinarum fabularum exempla, nedum Punicam Pœnuli orationem, librariorum inscitia et incuria, nævos contraxisse, sine antiquiorum meliorumque librorum auxilio, vix sanabiles;" and also, speaking of these verses, "Nonnulli versus ita comparati sunt, ut vulgatæ scripturæ neque medela, neque explicatio probabilis, inventa sit." To refer to the SECOND VERSE, "difficillimus omnium," as Gesenius calls it: of the forty-two letters of which it is composed, no less than twenty-one have been treated as spurious by the one or the other of these learned writers. By Bochart this line is read, CHI MELACHAI NITTHEMU MATSLIA MIDDABAREHEM ISKI: and by Gesenius, CHYM LACCHU YTH TUMMY

'STHYAL MYTTHIBARIIM ISCHI : the one translates it, " Ut consilia mea compleantur, prosperum sit ex ductu eorum negotium meum ;" the other, "Ut, ubi abstulerunt prosperitatem meam, impleatur, jussu eorum, desiderium meum,"

In attempting the interpretation of the TEN VERSES, I venture to controvert the received opinion of the learned; and to contend, that the substantial integrity of this portion of the existing copies of the Pœnulus has been unnecessarily, and unjustly, impugned by the critics.

The printed copies of the comedy are derived, we are told, from three manuscripts; to be found, one at Rome, another at Heidelberg, and the third at Leipsic. The text of the EDITIO PRINCEPS, printed at Venice in the year 1472, will be used for the purposes of the present investigation : it is said by Gesenius to approach most nearly to that of the LEIPSIC MS. According to this edition, the TEN VERSES contain three hundred and seventy-eight letters; and of these the mistakes imputable to the copyists affect, I would say, at the utmost, but eighteen; and in one instance only do the corrections they render necessary call for the rejection or change of more than a single letter of the word.

Moreover, the emendations proposed have little of a conjectural character, but appear to be clearly pointed to by the context: two of them are to be met with in the Roman MS., and another in the Plautus of Robert Stephens, dating in the year 1530. For instance, if, in the SECOND VERSE, we discard, with the Roman MS., the third CH, and change a succeeding T into an L, we regain, I imagine, the true reading of the line: CHYM-LACHUN YTH MUMYSLY ALMYCTHY BARIIIM ISCHI.

The corrections which the text of the EDITIO PRINCEPS appears to require will stand as follows, the FIRST and FIFTH VERSES being treated as absolutely intact.

Second Verse.

Reject CH, reading CHYMLACHUN (Roman MS.), for CHYMLACHCHUN; and change T into L, reading MUMYSLY for MUMYSTY.

Third Verse.

Insert R, reading LIPHORCAN for LIPHO-CAN.

Fourth Verse.

Reject R, reading BYN for BYRN.

Sixth Verse.

Change E into A, reading YSSIDA for YSSIDE; insert Y, reading YTHYFEL for THYFEL; and change U into E, reading LIPHEL for LIPHUL.

Seventh Verse.

Reject Y, reading DIBURTHI (Robert Stephens), for DIBURTHYI.

Eighth Verse.

Change H into Y, reading ELYCOTYS for ELY-COTHS.

Ninth Verse.

Change I into E, reading BYNNIED for BYN-NIID; change G into C, reading HILIC for HILIG; change U into Y, and N into M, reading UBYLIM for UBULIN (Roman MS. UBULIM); and insert E, reading ITTEHYM for ITTHYM.

Tenth Verse.

Reject Y, reading ALTHERA for ALYTHERA; reject U, reading YNNYNNYS for YNNYNNUYS; insert A, reading AMON for MON; and change H into I, reading COTI for COTH.

The amended text may be thus translated.

First Verse.

NOW, ON THE GODS AND THE GODDESSES OF THIS PLACE DO I CALL,

Second Verse.

TO PURGE AWAY MY STAINS, THAT SO I MAY BECOME A SPOTLESS MAN; TO

Third Verse.

QUICKLY BRING TO ME MY DAUGHTERS, MY DAUGHTERS, THE DELIGHT OF MY OLD AGE.

Fourth Verse.

SHOULD ONE OFFER THE GODS THAT GIVE INCREASE OF THE INCREASE THAT CAN'T BE ONE'S OWN?

Fifth Verse.

IF DEATH DIDN'T STAND IN MY WAY, I SHOULD LODGE AT ANTIDAMAS' HOUSE.

Sixth Verse.

OF THE TROOP THAT PERAMBULATE DARKNESS IS HE, THE HOSTS THAT IN DARKNESS HAVE HOMES:

Seventh Verse.

AND (AIN'T I SO TOLD?) AGORASTOCLES IS THE SON THAT LAMENTS HIM.

Eighth Verse.

I BRING WITH ME, SEE! 'TIS HIS GIFT, A GRAVING,
A CUT-IN-TWAIN GOD;

Ninth Verse.

A WITNESS 'TWIXT ME AND THE HOUSE-GODS, IF
HEAVEN HAS LED ME TOWARDS THEM.

Tenth Verse.

HERE I STAND 'MIDST THE CROWDS THAT PASS BY:
A LOT HAVE THEY 'MONGST THEM WHO FOREIGNERS
CANNOT ABIDE.

I proceed to exhibit the original and corrected
text of the Editio Princeps in three forms. First,
the letters of each verse will be set out in an un-
broken series, distinguishing, by asterisks placed over
them, such as are to be withdrawn from the line,
and including between brackets the letters to be
introduced into it. Next, the corrected contents of
the verse will be drawn from it, and distributed into
distinct words. Lastly, the amended text will be
transcribed in Hebrew letters, adding thereto the
points in the few cases where the pronunciation
differs from the received punctuation of the Hebrew.
To the production of this text some preliminary
observations will be necessary.

L

And, first. Although the contents of the TEN
VERSES satisfactorily establish the original identity
of the Carthaginian and Hebrew tongues, they yet
present us with some forms the use of which the
sacred writers have declined. We have, then, the
word אתי, existing as a pronoun of the first person
singular. The full form occurs in the first, second,
and eighth verses ; whilst as a suffix, תי, it is found
in the seventh. The undoubted derivation of the
second person singular of the past tense of the
Hebrew verb from the root, and a pronoun taking
the forms אַתָּה and אַתָּה, might lead us to conclude
that the first person singular of the same tense must
be a compound of the root and a pronoun, having
the forms אַתִּי, אתי; and the same pronoun may also
enter into the composition of the Hebrew objective
אותי. Since both אני and אתי appear to have been in
use amongst the Carthaginians, both are perhaps
contractions of a longer word, אָנְתִי. Next, we find
the verb with a prefixed ש; a form seemingly emphatic, and analogous to the shaphel of the Syriac.
It occurs in the first, and (as I think) in the sixth
verse also : in this last, however, the letters are susceptible of more than one interpretation. Then, we
have not only ל and של, but also ש used as signs of

the genitive; and in the sixth verse, where two geni-
tives come together, the first has the prefix שׁ, and
the other ל. The places of two nouns in the state
of definite construction are sometimes transposed,
and the noun in the genitive put first; but this, as,
also, the use of the construct for the absolute form
of the noun, may be regarded as poetical licences.
The feminine plural ends in ת; and the punctuation
of הוא, as a pronoun masculine of the third person,
is הוֹא. Lastly, a fondness for the vowel E appears;
whether this be a characteristic of the Phœnician
generally, or a peculiarity confined to the language
as spoken by the Carthaginians. Thus, we have
זֵאת for זאת; אֵפֵל for אפל; שֵׁרֵת for שָׁרֵת: (perhaps)
also, מֵחֹה for מָחֹה; and בֵּנוּת for בָּנוּת.

The form into which Plautus has thrown the
words of the original will also require attention.
Throughout these verses an initial י is treated by
the poet as a vowel, taking (so to speak) the sound
of the point attached to it; and, as with the Greeks,
the letter שׁ is always represented by the unaspirated
S. For שֵׁי, therefore, we have YS; for יְשָׁרֵת, ISY-
RYTH; IMLACH for יְמַלַח; ETHU for יֵתוּ; and
IS for אִישׁ. In most cases Y represents the TSERE of
the Hebrews, and is considered as equivalent to I. I:

as, YTH for אֶת; CHYMLACH for כִּרְיָמְלָח; and LYM for לִיאָם. The first verse comprises eighteen syllables, reduced, by the elision of three vowels, to fifteen, the average length of the Latin hexameter; and a determination that all the verses shall have the same length seems to be clearly evinced. To effect this, in the second verse a syllable is added to the word בָּרִים, which is here trisyllabic. In two instances a final י takes the form I. I; as BYNU-THII for בנותי, and OTHII for אותי. In the last case, this form appears to add a syllable to the word.

With these introductory remarks, I offer my reading of the TEN VERSES to the judgment of the learned.

First Verse.

N. Y. T. H. A. L. O. N. I. M. V. A. L. O. N. U.
T. H. S. I. C. O. R. A. T. H. I. S. I. M. A. C. O. M.
S. Y. T. H.

NYTH ALONIM VALONUTH SICORATHI SIMACOM SYTH.

נא את אלונים ואלונות שְׁקוֹרָא אֶתִי שמקום זֶאת

Second Verse.

C. H. Y. M. L. A. C. H. C̊. H̊. U. N. Y. T. H. M.

U. M. Y. S. †. [L.] Y. A. L. M. Y. C. T. H. I. B. A.
R. I. I. I, M. I. S. C. H. I.

CHYMLACHUN YTH MUMYSLY ALMYC-
THI BARIIIM ISCHI.

כי ימלחון את מומים יש לי על מחה אָתֵי בריים איש כי

Third Verse.

L. I. P. H. O. [R.] C. A. N. E. T. H. Y. T. H. B.
Y. N. U. T. H. I. I. A. D. A. E. D. I. N. B. Y. N.
U. T. H. I. I.

LIPHORCAN ETHYTH BYNUTHII AD'
AËDIN BYNUTHII.

לי פורחן יתו את בנותי עדי העדן בנותי

Fourth Verse.

B. Y. R. N. A. R. O. B. S. Y. L. L. O. H. O. M. A.
L. O. N. I. N. U. B. Y. M. I. S. Y. R. T. H. O. H. O.

'BYN AROB SYLLOHO 'MALONI NUBYM
ISYRTHOHO.

מבין הרוב של לא הוא אם אלוני נובים יְשֵׁרתו הוא

Fifth Verse.

B. Y. T. H. L. Y. M. M. O. T. H. Y. N. N. O. C.
T. O. T. H. I. I. V. E. L. E. C. A. N. T. I. D. A. S.
M. A. C. H. O. N.

BYTHLYM MOTHYN NOCTOTHII VELEC
ANTIDAS MACHON.

בית לי אם מות אין נחת אותי בהלך אנטידמס מכן

Sixth Verse.

Y. S. S. I. D. E̊. [A.] L. E. B. R. I. M. [Y.] T. H.
Y. F. E. L. Y. T. H. C. H. Y. L. Y. S. C. H. O. N. T.
H. E. M. L. I. P. H. Ů. [E.] L.

YSSIDA LEBRIM YTHYFEL YTHCHYLY
SCHONTHEM LIPHEL.

יש שעדה לעברים את אפל את חלי שקותים לאפל

Seventh Verse.

U. T. H. B. Y. N. I. M. Y. S. D. I. B. U. R. T. H.
Ẏ. I. N. N. O. C. U. T. H. N. U. A. G. O. R. A. S.
T. O. C. L. E. S.

UTHBYN IMYS DIBURTHI 'NNOCUTHNU
AGORASTOCLES.

ואת בן אם יש דברתי הנאקותינו אגורסטוקלס

Eighth Verse.

Y. T. H. E. M. A. N. E. T. H. I. H. Y. C. H. I. R.
S. A. E. L. Y. C. O. T. Ḣ. [Y.] S. I. T. H. N. A. S. O.

YTHE MANETHI HY CHIRSA ELYCOTYS
ITHNASO.

אתי מאנה אתי הא חרשה אליקוט יש אתנה שהוא

Ninth Verse.

B. Y. N. N. I. İ. [E.] D. C. H. I. L. L. L. U. H. I.
L. I. G̊. [C.] U. B. Ů. [Y.] L. I. Ṅ. [M.] L. A. S. I.
B. I. T. T. [E.] H. Y. M.

BYNNIED CHILLU HILIC UBYLIM LA-SIB' ITTEHYM.

בְּיּנִי עֵד כִּי אֵלוּ הֵילִיד וּבִין אֵלִים לְשִׁיבָה אֻתָּם

Tenth Verse.

B. O. D. Y. A. L. Y̊. T. H. E. R. A. Y. N. N. Y.
N. N. Ŭ. Y. S. L. Y. M. [A.] M. O. N. C. O. T. Ħ.
[I.] L. U. S. I. M.

BODY ALTHERA YNNYNNYS LYM AMON
COTILUSIM.

בְעֻדִים עַל תֵּרֵע הַגְּנִי יֵשׁ לָהֶם הַטֻּן קוּטִי לוּצִים

OBSERVATIONS.

FIRST VERSE.—ALONIM. אלונים and אלהים appear to be different forms of the same word, and to be derived from אל : אֵל־הוּא, MIGHTY-ONE; אֵלֹחַ, אֵלָה, אֵלוֹנִים, אֵלִיהִים. The terminations ה and ן are equivalents; so שְׁלֹמֹה, is written by the Septuagint translators Σαλωμων, or שִׁלְמֹן, that is, שָׁלוֹם־הוּא. MACOM. So Abraham uses מקום for עִיר (Gen. xviii. 24). It is singular that, with the story of Abdalonymus, as related by Quintus Curtius, before him, Bochart should insist on reading ELYON, in this verse, for

ALONIM. For ABDALONYM is עֶבֶד־אֱלוֹנִים, SERVUS DEORUM.

SECOND VERSE.—CHYMLACHUN. מלח, which in Ezekiel signifies *To rub with salt*, as part of the customary purifications of the new-born child, is here used in the sense of *purging*, or *purifying*, in general. An allusion to infant purity may, perhaps, be intended. So Shakspeare, "Till the foul deeds done in my course of nature are burnt and purged away." We have here the paragogic or emphatic וּ, following כִי; and the Moveable Sheva is represented (as is commonly the case in the Septuagint), by the letter A. MUMYSLY. The reading may be מוּמִי שְׁלִי; Hanno, perhaps, referring to some particular sin, punished by the gods with the loss of his daughters. ALMYCTHI. מחה has here the secondary signification observable in Numb. xxxiv. 11, *To reach to*, *To attain to*; and hence, as we say, *To be come*. BARIM. אִישׁ בָּרִים, the intensive plural of בּוֹר.

THIRD VERSE.—LIPHORCAN, An adverb פְרְחָן, or פְרְחָם, formed, I imagine, from the participle of פרח, and signifying, literally, *Flyingly*.

FOURTH VERSE.—SYLLOHO. שֶׁל לֹא הוּא, for לֹא שֶׁלּוֹ. "We have nothing," says Hanno, "but what has been given us by the gods; and to affect to give to them, when we can only do so out of their own gifts, is absurd. So David, " All things come of Thee; and of Thine own have we given Thee." (1 Chron. xxix. 14.) ISYRTHO. Piel of שׁרת, with the paragogic י, the occurrence of which in the Hebrew as an addition to the verb has been doubted.

SIXTH VERSE.—LEBRIM. עָבֵר, a verbal from עבר, and signifying, Passer-on, Pilgrim. It occurs in Gen. x. 21, where it has been mistaken for a proper-name: " Shem," says Moses, " was the father of all the בְּנֵי עֵבֶר, all the sons of ' Passing-on,' ' Pilgrimage;' all who, after the flood, betook themselves to the Nomadic life. Hence Abraham had the appellation העברי, THE HEBREW, THE PILGRIM, whether adopted by himself or bestowed on him by the Almighty; because, in obedience to the command of God, he entered on and endured a pilgrimage which was to end only with his life. SCHONTHEM. The text may be read, את חל יש קונתים.

SEVENTH VERSE.—'NNOCUTHNU. A verbal, as it seems, from נאק, and equivalent to נְאָקָה. The suffix may be the singular, נוּ; but it seems rather to be the plural נוּ; Hanno here using that jocular form of speaking which puts the plural for the singular; 'Our-sorrowing-son,' or, in the idiom of the Hebrew, 'The-son-of-our-sorrows.' That such method of expression is not inconsistent with the character, appears from the subsequent verses, in which the Carthaginian is made to say, speaking of his deceased friend Antidamas, 'Eum fecisse aiunt sibi quod faciendum fuit.'

EIGHTH VERSE.—CHIRSA. I take this to be חָרָשׁ with the emphatic ה postfixed. Other words derived to the Greeks from the Phœnicians exhibit the same formation: as אֵלָפֶה for הָאֵלֶף; נִבְלָה for תֵּבֶל. May not even אֱלוֹהַ be an example of the same form: אֵלְרָה for הָאֵלְדָא, THE-ALMIGHTY-ONE. CHIRSA ELYCOT: TESSARA DIMIDIATA: DEUS HOSPITALIS.

NINTH VERSE.—CHILLU. The force of כִּי appears to be lost, as in the כִּי אָם of the Hebrew. ITTEHYM. The punctuation of the Hebrew, and the consideration that without the inserted E the line would have but fourteen syllables, appear to warrant the addition of this letter, or the Moveable Sheva.

TENTH VERSE.—BODYM ALTHERA. 'The-goers-before-the-door,' the 'Passengers-in-the-streets.'

YNNYNNYS. The reading may be YNNYNU YSYLYM, הננו יש להם, as in the Editio Princeps; Hanno here including himself and his audience. If this reading be adopted, the A, inserted to complete the number of syllables, must be withdrawn; and we must read 'MON for AMON.

The similarity of structure observable in the Carthaginian of Hanno and the Hebrew of Moses and the Prophets, sufficiently identifies both languages with the Phœnician; and the identity of the Phœnician and the Hebrew tongues established, it follows, that the Israelites received their language from the descendants of Canaan, the son of Ham; and that the Hebrew of the Bible is no other than the Canaanitish, or Phœnician, tongue, expressed in the Chaldaic character, the character brought (we may well believe) by Abraham himself from Ur of the Chaldees. But the books of Moses offer us evidence, hardly to be resisted, that the language of his writings was, also, the language of the Antediluvian World; and hence it follows, further, that in the grand confusion of languages at Babel the primitive tongue was continued to mankind in the line of Canaan; and so, by a circuitous providence, the language spoken by the SECOND ADAM was (in the

main) the language of THE FIRST. The Scriptures
afford no countenance to the philology which aims
at establishing the original identity of all languages,
and reproducing the common mother of them all,
the tongue spoken by Noah when he issued from the
ark. They teach us that human speech is not derived from one, but many mothers; mothers created
(with one exception) in the same hour; standing
towards each other in the relationship of sisters;
and holding, therefore, amongst themselves, equal
and independent rank. The Syriac, Chaldee, and
Arabic, may be derivatives from the Phœnician, and
may owe their existence to the great outspread of
Canaan's sons, (Gen. x. 18); or they may be primitive and distinct tongues, designed by their Creator
to evince how near in structure one language may
approach another, and yet the end of their creation
be obtained, and the speakers of them be unintel-
ligible to each other. (Isa. xxvi. 11; Jer. v. 15.)

The TEN VERSES afford an argument, conclusive
against the system of those Hebraists who deny the
authenticity of the pronunciation preserved and
perpetuated by the Masoretic punctuation of the
Hebrew Scriptures, and greatly in favour of the
origin and antiquity attributed to 'the points' by

the tradition of the Jews. 'The points,' say the
Jews, 'were from Moses; but were first added to
the letters by Ezra:' (in other words) The pronunciation of the Hebrew indicated by the Masoretic
punctuation is as old as Moses, and was, indeed,
'from the beginning;' but 'the points' by which it
has been derived to us were excogitated, and first
added to the letters, by this great scribe. How
slight the difference between the pronunciation of
the Phœnician, as spoken at Carthage in the days of
Plautus, and that delivered to us by the Punctuists
as the pronunciation of the Hebrew in the times of
Dido and the Israelitish kings!

CORRIGENDA.

Page 12, line 21—*for* comminuat, *read* comminuet.

Page 41, line 23—*for* Lycophron of Cassandra, *read* Cassandra of Lycophron.

Page 62, line 15—*for* שְׁלִי־אֵל, *read* שָׁלֵת־יְ־אֵל.

Page 75, line 14—*for* other words, *read* other verbs of this class.

Page 78, lines 11 and 12—*for* I-MUST-BE, *read* I MUST BE; *and for* HE-MUST-BE, *read* HE MUST BE.

Page 87, line 13—*for* תְּרֹרֶיָה, *read* תְּרֹעֶיָה.

Page 88, line 7—*for* punctum-glutationis, *read* punctum-glutinationis.

LONDON:

PRINTED BY WILLIAM CLOWES AND SONS,
STAMFORD STREET.

CPSIA information can be obtained
at www.ICGtesting.com
Printed in the USA
BVHW030257240621
610023BV00003B/83